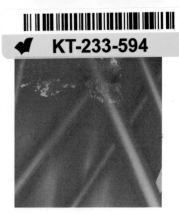

Creating connections:

college innovations in flexibility, access
and participation

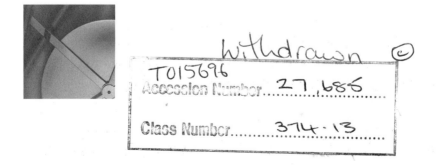

Creating connections: college innovations in flexibility, access and participation

Published by the Further Education Development Agency (FEDA) and the Association of Colleges (AoC).

Further Education Development Agency (FEDA)

Coombe Lodge, Blagdon, Bristol BS18 6RG

Tel: 01761 462503   Fax: 01761 463140

Registered with the Charity Commissioners

Association of Colleges (AoC)

7/8 Rathbone Place, London, W1P 1DE

Tel: 0171 6373919   Fax: 0171 631 0918

Cover and pages designed by Mike Pope, FEDA

Edited by Jennifer Rhys, FEDA

Publication management by Ann-Marie Warrender, FEDA

Printed by Henry Ling Limited, Dorchester

Cover photograph: Telegraph Colour Library

ISBN 1 85338 434 8

© 1996 FEDA and AoC

Foreword

'Only connect...' E.M. Forster

This book tells the story of the Fairbairn Fellowship project. It is a learning adventure story, not a dry account of curricular research in FE. Whether you are interested in the management of major projects, creating access to opportunities for learning, the enabling role of new technology, or the way in which the FE sector responds to a challenge, you should read this book and reflect upon its conclusions.

Ruth Gee's opening chapter sets out what we did and how we did it — and what has been learned from the three years' experience. Resources are not enough: you also need a clear vision and adequate time to achieve success. Ursula Howard's closing chapter evaluates the project, and draws attention to eight key issues which emerge — such as the importance of basic principles, effective management, co-operation, and staff capability. In between, the 12 Fairbairn Fellows tell their own stories of what they intended, achieved and learned. It is a moving and impressive tale.

Creating Connections shows how much can be done with quite a small investment of funds. The Esmée Fairbairn Charitable Trust has reason to feel well pleased with the results of its first substantial venture into the world of FE. The success of this project throws down a challenge to other Trusts — and to other sectors of education. But the real test will be in the years to come, as colleges throughout the FE sector build on what is set out here to increase flexibility, access and participation. I am sure they will.

Sir Christopher Ball
Chairman, Fairbairn Fellowship Steering Committee

iii

Acknowledgements

The Association for Colleges (AfC) was established in 1993 to support and promote further education colleges throughout the UK. In its inaugural year, the Association made a successful bid to the Esmée Esmée Fairbairn Charitable Trust and received a grant of £720,000 over a three year period.

In August 1996, the Association for Colleges merged with the Colleges Employers Forum to become the Association of Colleges (AoC).

The Association would like to acknowledge the support and assistance of the Steering Group members and our partners´ — The Staff College and the Further Education Unit (FEU) which merged to become the Further Education Development Agency (FEDA) from April 1995.

Steering Group Membership: December 1993-December 1996

- Sir Christopher Ball (Chair)

- Stephen Crowne, Chief Executive, FEDA (from April 1995)

- Kevin Donovan, Head of Technology and Management of Learning, FEDA

- Ruth Gee, Chief Executive, Association for Colleges

- Ursula Howard, Director of Research & Information, FEDA (from April 1995)

- Chris Hughes, Principal, Gateshead College

- Geoff Melling, Chief Executive, The Staff College (until April 1995)

- Judith Norrington, Director of Curriculum and Quality, Association of Colleges

- Geoff Stanton, Director, FEU (until April 1995)

c r e a t i n g   c o n n e c t i o n s

Contents

Chapter 1
Leading from the front — a steering group perspective

Ruth Gee

What follows is a story; the story of what we did and how we did it, then on reflection how we might do it now if we were to do the same thing again. We hope that we can help others learn from our experience and identify some general lessons on project management for us all.

There are three distinct parts to our work I shall describe: first how we conceived and selected the Fellowships; secondly, how we managed the work, and finally how we sought to capture the benefits for the sector as a whole and disseminate the lessons learnt. The Fellows describe in their own chapters the delivery and outcomes of individual Fellowships.

Conception and selection — what is the vision?

It is important to remember the context in which the Association for Colleges application to the Esmée Fairbairn Trust took place.

While colleges had been making a positive contribution to their local communities for many years, it was only when they were incorporated in April 1993 that there was a real opportunity to create a public perception of a national 'further education (FE) sector'. Traditionally acknowledged within the profession and elsewhere as the 'Cinderella service', FE colleges have much to contibute to the economic well-being and benefit of society, as an increasing number of politicians and policy makers began to realise. The Association for Colleges (AfC) was formed in early 1993 to promote and support colleges, increase their public identity and help exchange good practice in an increasingly competitive world. It is owned by the colleges to act for the colleges.

Prior to 1993, through no fault of the colleges, there had been little participation in national policy development. Individual local education authorities (LEAs) controlled the policy, administration and practice of the colleges and there was a lack of coherent national policy. Within that framework it was hardly surprising that there was an absence of national information about what colleges were doing and why they were doing it. Research of any kind, basic or strategic, was practically unknown.

The Council/Board of the AfC and its officers had a vision: they wished to gain new and additional private resources to enable the sector to innovate in ways which could not be achieved through the public purse, making appropriate use of the enormous potential of increasingly accessible information technology (IT).

The vision was an ambitious one. It sought to use the traditional strengths of the colleges: their diversity (reflecting their location, curriculum and physical infrastructure); their responsiveness to local needs (traditionally through strong links with employers); and their inclusive approach to enrolment. While school sixth forms and universities select, colleges embrace an open-door policy of welcoming learners regardless of ability, age, sex, disability and mode of study. It is worth remembering that there are more students in FE colleges today than in all school sixth forms and universities combined.

So the AfC sought to utilise these traditional strengths and encourage the development of a high profile curriculum development 'initiative' which would build an identifiable individual expertise in colleges (the Fellows). It would embed best practice at a local level, and at the same time generate national awareness, and assist national strategies to ensure the continuation of innovation and professionalism.

While I might use the word 'project' in describing our work, we intended always that the Fairbairn Fellows' work should be of national significance with long-term practical implications. Although individual college projects might be relatively small-scale, they had to be an integral part of the college's strategic plan and they had to have potential large-scale implications. It was an AfC ambition from the outset to embed our work in the best practice of the 1990s and beyond.

Application

For these reasons the AfC wished to involve other partners in the FE sector. While we recognise the value and importance of operating in a competitive environment, we also believe that collaboration is essential.

Some of the useful lessons from the private sector have been about 'competitive collaboration'. There were two key players at the time. One, The Staff College was supported primarily by LEAs and individual colleges for the development and delivery of a professional and personal development and training. The other, the Further Education Unit (FEU), also funded through the public purse, focused on aspects of curriculum development and stimulated action research in specific curriculum areas. We were fortunate in that both organisations valued our prospective contribution to the sector, and agreed to support our application to the Esmée Fairbairn Trust. The AfC has provided the overall leadership and strategic drive of the enterprise, and covered the related costs, but the partnership model was explicit in the application and our subsequent way of working.

There was no history of applications to a private trust for money to be used to the benefit of the public education sector, and we were anxious to demonstrate our capacity to work collaboratively to provide for innovation which could not otherwise take place. In fact that proved to be an essential prerequisite for the Trustees. We were successful in obtaining a grant of £720,000 only because the Trustees were supportive of our vision and satisfied with our business plan. FEU agreed to monitor the progress of selected projects through its regional officers. The Staff College agreed to provide a residential conference twice a year for all those involved.

It was unusual for FEU to monitor programmes which were not its own, and it has been an interesting exercise observing the strengths and weaknesses of this model during the implementation process. More of that later when I turn to the management of the scheme. The bid to the Trust was also unusual in that it sought to fund individual Fellows within colleges.

As there was an absence of strategic research in the FE sector, so there was a lack of recognition for the individual practitioner, the teaching staff member, and the professional whom so many students had privately thanked and acknowledged. While the university sector celebrates its academics, flaunting academic freedom as a barrier to institutional leadership and managerialism, the FE colleges have no such history. The introduction of the Fellowships was a visionary approach, designed to acknowledge that within the colleges, too, individuals could contribute at a corporate and national level to the development of best practice. Equally importantly, they deserved to be recognised.

In inviting colleges to apply for funds we asked them to identify a suitable individual, or job share, and provide details of their c.v.(s). Our priority was to appoint strong professionals within good colleges, whose leadership would encourage, stimulate and develop the initiatives, thus adding at an institutional level to the framework provided by regional FEU officers and the national steering group.

The ultimate aim, of course, was that college students would be beneficiaries: through our endeavours we hoped that individuals would enjoy easier access, improved attainment, and more positive outcomes. Ideally we hoped it would be possible for the individual student to enjoy all three. The outcomes described by the Fellows demonstrate the success of that ambition as hundreds of students have participated who would not otherwise have done so.

It was important that the scope of the scheme should be UK-wide. While there are different legislative structures for FE in England, Wales, Scotland and Northern Ireland, we wanted to make the point that good professional practice transcends structural differences.

In describing our vision, we hoped to appeal to our benefactors and were delighted when in September 1993 we were able to announce to the press, public and the professionals our ability to translate a vision into reality.

On reflection, we would adopt the same approach again.

Lessons

- *Have a clear vision.*
- *Think nationally as well as locally — aim high.*
- *Select partners with whom to collaborate.*
- *Target your audience in order to achieve results.*

Selecting projects

My early training for equal opportunities employment selection, taught me that the job interview is the last part of a process and not the first. The establishment of criteria, the mapping and weighting of them, and the other front-end loaded procedures are the essential ingredients for a positive conclusion. Programmes like this are the same. The marketing brochure set out the main task of the Fellows as 'the development of the FE curriculum utilising new ideas of flexible learning and modern learning technology so as to help achieve measurable increases in participation, attainment, and learning productivity'.

While it gives examples of the kind of work that might be supported, and while I believe that was sufficient for the marketing brochure, I do not believe the Steering Committee had shared its own values and aspirations in sufficient detail for the final selection criteria to be specific enough.

The applications fell into a number of broad themes — access, technology, curriculum materials development, and special needs. They were self-defining themes from which applicants believed our aims of increased participation, attainment and learning productivity would result.

On reflection I think we ought to have spent longer as a steering group clarifying our objectives, weighting their importance, cross-referencing the applicants, their theme and their regional profile. There is always a tendency to confuse the immediate with the urgent and our steering group may have fallen into the same trap. Rushed by a desire to begin work in January 1994, we had little time to publish details to colleges, receive and consider applications, select and initiate the Fellowships.

We ought to have considered the importance of a three-year scheme and its many ramifications in greater detail than we did. While our combined professional judgements have delivered successful outcomes, they may prove less than we had the opportunity to achieve.

On reflection we ought not to have allowed the thrust of the urgent to overcome the needs of the important considerations.

There were lessons on the administrative side, too. A simple time-saving and cost-effective measure would have been to ask each applicant to send in multiple copies of their bid. This has been done subsequently with positive results. Far better to have 200 applicants send in five copies than find yourself doing 800 photocopies!

If you are an organisation unused to sending out one message and receiving multiple replies, be prepared. You need to be prepared to deal with the additional post and initial sorting into regions. It takes time and we didn't 'cost' it sufficiently. We were a new national organisation at the time!

The selection panel received the bids one week before its meeting — the pre-meeting reading this allows is essential.

One of the selection panel members was absent due to a family bereavement. We might have postponed the panel and proceeded later at full strength rather than allowing urgency to dominate the proceedings. One key question is — would the outcome have been different? If a mapping of the applicants, analysis of their strengths and weaknesses and list of recommendations had been circulated in advance, then the answer is probably no. But in deference to the intellects of the panel members and the need for speed, this was not done and the reality is that we will never know!

The importance of the selection criteria is paramount. We were deliberate, for our own internal reasons, about selecting one bid from each region. We wished to demonstrate an even-handedness, to demonstrate that we were not regionally biased in any way. This may have distorted the outcome and resulted in the selection of some projects in preference to others simply because the weight of bids received was not equitable. Also some regions are much bigger than others.

Also, on reflection we might have clarified in advance whether we wished to acknowledge existing good practice and develop it, or to acknowledge and develop potential. In the event we went for a mixture of the two.

This has implications for the quality benchmark of the individual scheme. We wished to identify practitioners capable of being future national leaders and it still remains to be seen if this is the case. We ought not to be too self-critical, however, as there has been a climate of change within colleges between 1993 and 1996 which has made the relationship between teaching staff, middle managers and senior managers very complex.

The 'contracts' debate may well have affected the development of the scheme in a number of ways. First, a reluctance from those teaching Fellows selected to embrace leadership roles. None were designated senior staff and in some colleges there was a reluctance to embrace additional managerial functions once the conflict culture became more widespread. Secondly, there might have been a reluctance by chief executives and corporations to view individuals with curriculum expertise as having core managerial potential. It has been a period when curriculum strength has been put in a secondary position to resource and budgetary expertise, or to human resource, estates or other specialist expertise. That may have been an inevitable consequence of incorporation, which imposed new demands in these areas. While the core business of providing first-class education remained the most important task, some colleges allowed the urgent to distract them from the important.

creating connections

The success of the scheme depends, at least in part, on the college's ability not only to include the Fellowship within its strategic plan, but also to integrate its delivery within 'mainstream objectives'. We have had some experience of college management teams initially paying only token recognition to the value of the Fellowship. We had to be prepared to intervene, to remind college chief executives that this was a condition of funding and also in the college's best long-term interests.

The steering group's ambiguity about the status of the Fellows — real or potential — affected the Fellows' own sense of self worth. We wished to empower all Fellows to become institutional and national leaders in their field. In some cases this is demonstrable; in others the proof remains to be seen. The steering group has worked hard to achieve this with much work done on performance indicators, threshold benchmarks and quality assessment but we ought to be able to be 100% confident that all Fellows feel of value and national importance. Have they been genuinely empowered and fulfilled? Only they can say.

Lessons

- *Don't confuse the urgent with the important.*
- *Build in sufficient time to administer the pre-selection process.*
- *Officers should circulate recommended applications in advance to panel members.*
- *Every steering group member needs to have ample opportunity to read the documentation in advance of the selection meeting. Don't leave them until you are on the journey to the meeting.*
- *Ease the administrative burden by asking applicants to submit multiple copies.*
- *Try to ensure that all participants have a sense of their value and the importance of their contribution.*

- *A steering group needs to be willing and able to give support and guidance to individuals regardless of their role. It is important for chief executives as well as individuals participating at the ground level.*

- *College corporations should recognise when a college has been successful in attracting external money.*

- *Colleges should celebrate their own success and that of the individuals involved by celebrating the importance of the achievements both internally and externally.*

- *Special projects should be an integral part of a college's strategic plan.*

Delivering and disseminating the project

Teamwork is essential. We determined in advance the respective roles of the AfC as programme leaders, managers and administrators, with The Staff College and FEU (FEDA) offering ongoing professional support to individual Fellows and the steering group. That has worked well and led to a model collaborative arrangement.

It is significant that after 16 months of operation, FEU and The Staff College were closed and the Government set up a new body, the Further Education Development Agency (FEDA). Two important steering group members were replaced by new FEDA personnel, neither of whom had been involved with either of the predecessor organisations. It is a credit to the individuals involved and the robustness of the project infrastructure that the project nationally has withstood these changes.

FEDA designs and manages its own programmes but also works in collaboration with other organisations. For this project a new orientation was necessary. FEDA's regional officers, briefed about the project and meeting regularly as a team throughout its lifetime, supported the Fellows in a number of ways. They attended college steering group meetings, discussed developments with Fellows, offered information and advice, and monitored progress against targets on behalf of the national steering group, and in conjunction with AfC staff. Their enthusiasm for the project was evident throughout.

There have also been some invaluable lessons emanating from the residential conferences which took place twice a year. They gave the steering group an opportunity to get to know the Fellows, as well as the opportunity for the Fellows to get to know each other. Social and informal contact as well as the more structured part of the programme helped meet the objective of team-building at all the interfaces. There were a number of practical consequences, including the introduction of a Fellows' newsletter and the use of the AfC e-mail system for the maintenance of the network.

Within the management of the residential events, the steering group tried to devolve responsibility for programming to the Fellows. This seemed important to us as a part of their professional development. It has become clear that some Fellows adopt the leadership role more easily than others, that all are capable of it, and that they share a real desire to work collaboratively. All the projects are self-contained in their own right and yet we have tried to manage them as a totality. In many respects this mirrors the FE sector as a whole in that they reflect the diversity of the sector in their purpose and their mode of delivery. The original version of partnership has proved its value.

Lessons

- *There is a need to be clear about individual steering group members' roles. The steering group needs to have a clear perspective on who is responsible for what.*
- *Be prepared to intervene as and when necessary.*
- *Use informal as well as formal methods of networking.*

Dissemination

AfC recognised at the outset the need to take legal advice about intellectual property rights and its specific relevance to the Fellowship. It was agreed that all commercial benefits of the work should be enjoyed and shared by the whole sector, rather than individual colleges and indeed, this was a condition of funding. Every college was required to sign a letter undertaking that any commercial benefits should be shared. This is important as it recognises the role of the 'benefactor' in seeking to assist the whole sector rather than individual colleges. At this stage it is clear that there is the potential to develop commercial prototypes but the scale of the operation is unknown. Some colleges have developed projects like CD-ROMs which they are using internally but have the potential for national sales.

Commercial significance is just one reason why dissemination of the project is important. We agreed in advance that dissemination of the work should be ongoing and not confined to a final end of programme 'grand slam'. We have therefore used the twice-yearly residential not only as an opportunity to spread inter-Fellow collegiality, to develop the relationship between the steering group and the Fellows, but also to agree the contemporary message and how to spread it.

In Glasgow in 1994 and London 1995, the Fellows mounted an exhibition and presented a seminar. In Cardiff in 1996, the chair of the steering group will deliver a keynote address and the Fellows will exhibit their project outcomes as part of an extended educational market-place. There have been regular features in the AfC's newspaper *FE Now!* and at the AfC Annual Conference. Individual colleges have sought press and media coverage and some have attracted additional funding for local publicity, and the production of videos and other material.

While individual colleges and their students have acquired individual benefits — as described in the following chapters — we need also to try to assess the impact of the scheme as a whole. We have acknowledged the value of conducting a market poll amongst colleges to discover how far the programme is first recognised, and second, acknowledged for its importance. Until we do that it is difficult to measure its impact although the numbers and perspectives of students involved is a key indicator.

We ought also to conduct a questionnaire among the Fellows and the college senior management to get their views. We intend to do this beyond the end of the three-year funding period. I suspect we ought to have had more personal contact with the college principals involved and interviewed them in advance of the final selection outcome. We have reason to believe that at least half may have seen this work as less significant than we would have liked, and not fully thought through the implications of their involvement.

The Association for Colleges has successfully proposed a merger with the Colleges Employers Forum and with effect from August 1996 became part of the Association of Colleges. It is a testimony to the energy, enthusiasm and professionalism of all those involved that a major part of the dissemination of the Fellows' work will be undertaken by a new organisation some three years after the original AfC vision was recognised and rewarded by the Esmée Fairbairn Charitable Trust.

Lessons

- *Plan for long-term commercial and legal situations from the outset.*
- *Pace dissemination throughout and beyond the period of project funding.*
- *Use different methods to suit different audiences.*
- *Build in resilience and quality standards which can cope with externally imposed change.*
- *Keep your mind on the original vision and your voice on the achieved outcomes.*

Conclusions

Despite the lack of a substantial evaluation process, there are a number of conclusions the steering group feels able to make from its own involvement and observations. As well as the emergence of a number of key themes, notably flexibility, increased participation and the underlying importance of new technology in helping access, there are a number of generic lessons which we should note.

- systematic staff development reaps rewards for both staff and students
- team working provides value-added benefits to staff and students
- people matter; individuals can make a difference
- student demand can be stimulated through innovative local action
- IT is a key component of all project delivery
- IT cannot succeed alone; it needs human resources too
- management vision and support improve the delivery and achievements of individual projects
- local projects have national and international spin-offs
- small sums of money generate and attract larger sums from a variety of sources

We suspect but cannot prove that lives have been changed. The case studies provide a flavour. At least I believe we can claim that the work has made a difference. We should be encouraged that relatively small sums of money, £20,000 per college per year, have provided opportunities for students and college developments that would not have otherwise taken place.

Acknowledgements

Particular thanks should go to John Bevan, OBE, who submitted the original application for funds, and to Sir Christopher Ball, Chair of the steering group who supported the application, the AfC Council, Geoff Melling and Geoff Stanton who led the strategic planning, and Judith Norrington and Kevin Donovan who lived and breathed the oversight of practice.

FEDA's establishment in 1995 led to the helpful involvement of Stephen Crowne and Ursula Howard from summer 1995, and the staff at Blagdon and FEDA regional officers have been supportive throughout.

The hard work and expertise of the Fellows speak for themselves.

Ultimate thanks must go to the Esmée Fairbairn Charitable Trust, without whom none of this work would have been possible.

Ruth Gee
Chief Executive, Association for Colleges

Chapter 2
Access enabled?

Alison Cox

Stevenson College, Edinburgh

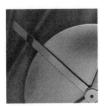

Introduction

If it has taken three years to conclude that the answer is:

It helps if you provide local, responsive and user-friendly access to relevant, up-to-date information, equipment and advice...

Then what was the question?

There are countless possibilities and the creative reader is probably toying with options such as 'how one might encourage more children to use libraries' or perhaps 'how to entice unfit adults to utilise the community sports facilities'.

In the case of the Scottish Fairbairn Fellowship, the pressing question was this:

Is it feasible to level the educational playing field for students with disabilities by exploiting the potential of 'technology'?

For more than a decade, staff at Stevenson College in Edinburgh, like many others in similar settings, have been seeking the definitive solution. Yet the ground under this educational playing field has been constantly shifting! The technology of 1996 and beyond bears little resemblance to the 'new technology' of yesteryear. If proof were ever needed that the last decade has witnessed rapid technological change, one need look no further than the first computing equipment order raised by the special educational needs staff at Stevenson College in the early 1980s:

Six BBC microcomputers with 40/80 switchable disk drives and 'green screen' monitors.

The latest word in information technology at the time — and yet now consigned to the category of 'museum pieces'!

There need be no embarrassment in sharing this information. As recently as 1982, *The Times* reported a newly published British opinion poll which revealed that 80% of those interviewed had not yet heard of information technology. In 1985, Michael Behrmann wrote:

Widespread application of high technology often lags behind the cutting edge of research and development. This is particularly true in education. The major factors constraining the application of technology appear to be financial (funding limitations), ideological (resistance to change) and experiential (resistance to learning about technology). Traditionally, once technological innovations penetrated education, the last population to benefit was the disabled.

In the latter regard, the situation has been partially addressed. There are examples of real 'technological trailblazing' by students with disabilities and their tutors, but have the constraining factors to which Behrmann refers now been lifted? Generally, is the climate in FE today very different from that of 1985?

At Stevenson College, the Fairbairn Fellowship has afforded the opportunity to ask questions, disseminate the answers and hopefully address some of the issues in practice — and in doing so, has shared the vision of 'developing approaches to learning which contribute to measurable increases in participation, attainment and learning productivity'.

The project

Since the project began, a key priority has been to focus on student perceptions of the ways in which technology has enhanced, or could enhance, their learning experiences. Through the use of semi-structured interviews, a wealth of data was obtained about the role played by enabling technology in the learning experiences of the students involved in the study. A summary of the interview schedule is contained in Figure 2.1 (see page 21).

From the evidence which those students have provided, and with reference to the views of tutors and technicians whose involvement in the whole process is so crucial, a picture has begun to take shape. Figure 2.2 (see page 22) attempts to represent the picture as a series of messages and ideas about the use of enabling technology in the learning environment.

Given that the issues faced by one FE college may have much in common with those faced by others, and that the intention of the Fairbairn Fellowships has been to encourage a free exchange of ideas, it

Touch screen interaction

is hoped that these messages might also inform the strategic planning process in other colleges.

The picture emerging from the Scottish Fairbairn study was used as a central theme for a national conference in May 1996, entitled 'Wider Still'. 'Wider Still' brought together delegates from schools, colleges, universities and advisory bodies with policy makers and funding

creating connections

Students' perceptions of technology

The term 'assistive technology' refers to computers and other equipment which are intended to compensate for any difficulties which may exist in the learning situation for students with disabilities.

Do you use any assistive technology in the course of your studies?	Would you like to describe what you use? Do you use this technology in all aspects of your course? How does this technology assist you?
When did you first start using this assistive technology?	How did you decide what to use? How did you acquire the technology, and how is it funded? Were you familiar with the technology before you started your course?
How did you learn about using the technology?	Did you have any training in how to use it? If so, who provided that training? If not, do you feel training would have been useful?
Have you experienced any difficulties with this assistive technology?	If so, would you like to describe what those difficulties have been? Who did you turn to for assistance? If you feel you did not receive adequate assistance, what further help would you have liked?
How important is this technology to you as a student?	Does the technology do everything you need it to do? What other factors currently help in your course? Are there other things that you feel would assist you if they were made available?

What messages have emerged from the study?	Who is the message for?
Portability and durability of equipment could be improved. Much of the available technology is not robust enough to withstand the frequent manoeuvring demanded by true integration into a typical college day.	• Equipment manufacturers • College facilities managers • Technical support staff
Reviews of policy regarding the college-wide provision of technology should always include representation from staff and/or student(s) experienced in disability access issues. Circulating a final draft of a policy document for comment is too little, too late.	• College senior managers • Computer services/IT managers • Students and advisers
Ongoing technical support and maintenance should be considered an integral part of equipment provision. Current funding strategies often overlook this requirement, accounting for initial purchase cost only.	• Funding councils • College finance directors
Gaining return for one's effort is important. 'Enabling' technology is at its best when maximum gain is derived with minimum exertion or hassle. This is not an indication of laziness on the part of the user but a reflection of the extensive demands on the energies of teachers and learners.	• Software designers • Technical publishers • Hardware manufacturers
Resource/IT centres for multiple group usage are becoming popular. If these centres are to be truly accessible to all users, the issue of equipment compatibility must be addressed. 'Enabling' devices can only be effective if they are compatible with a centre's computer workstations.	• IT managers • Resources centre planners • Learning support co-ordinators
Electronic superhighways offer exciting opportunities to participate in learning. It is crucial that superhighway routes are accessible and barriers are avoided. No student wants to be left in the slow lane!	• Internet providers • Web sponsors • Web Site developers
Staff development in effectively supporting learners with additional needs is not always given high enough priority. Much familiarisation with technology is done informally by staff in their own time. Cutting back on staff development is a false economy.	• TECs/LECs • Education departments • College senior managers
Supplying enabling technology should be regarded as a dynamic process, not an event. Learners' needs change and the available technology must reflect this. Progress might be be made through the creation of more regional resource banks — perhaps sponsored by industry.	• Large companies • Community investors • Charitable trusts

agencies to explore the issues challenging all who seek to create an inclusive, positive environment for learners with disabilities or additional support needs. A full report of the conference proceedings and a set of recommendations has been published by the Scottish Further Education Unit, *Wider Still: An Agenda for Action* (1996).

The three main aims of the Fairbairn Fellowship at Stevenson College have been to:

- encourage students with disabilities to participate in post-school education through the creation of a positive and supportive learning environment

- evaluate the role of technology in enabling students with disabilities to reach their potential

- consider the experiences of students with disabilities who are 'in transition' between sectors — for example, from school to FE, or from FE to HE — and to develop a resource to assist that transition process

The use of a general term such as 'students with disabilities' is open to wide interpretation. Any one study would be unlikely to encapsulate the varying needs of all individuals who might be represented by this phrase. In this project, the students who have been involved have physical or sensory disabilities, or specific learning difficulties (e.g. dyslexia). They have not been regarded as an homogenous group, but as individuals with different needs and expectations. This individuality means that an isolated case study could not do justice to these students, the staff or the technology.

The chart in Figure 2.2 is intended to summarise the issues and ideas which have emerged from the Fairbairn activities. There is always a risk that such a chart oversimplifies the picture, or loses the project's dynamism. For that reason, some of the quotes and comments from students and lecturers involved in the study have been included in the following pages.

Today's lessons in planning for tomorrow's technology

Computers make a positive contribution but they are not a cure-all!

Almost without exception, the students involved in the Fairbairn project said that they were pleased to have access to computers and other technological aids to learning. When asked why, there was a wide range of answers:

'My work looks much better when it is word-processed.'

'I don't get so tired if I'm using a computer for writing.'

'I couldn't do the course without this equipment (voice-activated computer) because my hands don't work.'

'I'm more confident because I can easily check my spelling before I hand in the assignment.'

'I can't see the text, so the computer reads everything back to me.'

Staff were also keen to use technology in supporting and enhancing learning:

'Once I discovered how to use the special software, it was amazing how well it enabled the student to keep up in class. It was a bit embarrassing that she knew more than I did about it at first!'

'I wish I'd known about this software ages ago. It's been around for a while and I could have been learning how to get the best from it.'

'I know other mainstream lecturers, like myself, who have been pleasantly surprised about how many good devices are available to support blind students. I don't read braille, yet I can turn my notes accurately into braille using a scanner and a translation package.'

So why isn't the computer a 'cure-all' solution? Students were also asked if there was anything computers couldn't do to assist their learning. The replies were quite revealing:

> 'The machine doesn't explain things. It just does what I tell it, so if I give it a wrong instruction it still does it!'

> 'I came to college for the social life as well as the education. Computers are lousy companions!'

> 'If I had to choose between computers and lecturers, I think the lecturers are more important because they listen and try to understand.'

> 'I'm sure computers can do most things. I wish there was a package that showed you everything they could do.'

As far as the staff were concerned, were there any limitations in the technology?

> 'The time it takes to get to know the technology isn't recognised. We can only use the technology fully if more development time is made available.'

> 'Doing this work on computer has probably taken longer than if we'd managed without — but the result is better.'

> 'I worry that disabled students can be isolated by the technology because they are surrounded by equipment instead of human help.'

> 'Computers will never replace teachers, but I hope using computers makes classes more interesting.'

> 'Technology changes so fast. I worry we are not giving students the latest versions of everything. Anyway, is the latest version always the best one?'

So, after three years is it possible to respond to the question posed early in the chapter?

Is it feasible to level the educational playing field for students with disabilities by exploiting the potential of 'technology'?

And what about those barriers of **funding limitations, resistance to change** and **resistance to learning about technology** to which Michael Behrmann alluded?

The answer?

The Scottish Fairbairn project assisted approximately 200 students with disabilities over the three years and that number is set to escalate with the circulation of the Access-Enabled resource pack.

The strongest message to come from the project is that 'having access to up-to-date information, and to advice and support, is as important as having access to technology'. The good news is that 'technophobia' is diminishing rapidly and being replaced by guarded enthusiasm.

An increasing availability of technology, and the recent introduction of disability discrimination legislation, are likely to raise both staff and students' expectations of what should be available and ought to be provided.

In this age of global communication, advanced information technology and access to electronic superhighways, it should be feasible to remove most barriers to participation in learning. However, it is important that the 'information' aspect of information technology is not swamped by the 'technology' component!

Boxes of hardware and stacks of computer software only enhance the curriculum and empower staff and students when the investment in 'kit' is matched by an investment in the users. Appropriate training, staff development and the introduction of a cohesive strategy are vital.

Given adequate resources, the FE sector probably has the greatest potential amongst education providers to offer meaningful learning opportunities to those whose needs are most effectively met in a flexible, responsive and non-threatening environment.

Fellows, and the colleges that have benefited from Fairbairn funding, share the responsibility with policy makers and funders for ensuring that this potential is fully realised!

The responses and experiences of staff and students have formed the basis for the development of an interactive CD-based resource pack providing information and advice for students with disabilities and their advisers. This resource pack is available to staff and students in, or linking with, further education.

Alison Cox is the Access Centre Manager at Stevenson College, Edinburgh.

References

Behrmann, Michael **Handbook of Microcomputers in Special Education**, NFER-Nelson Co. Ltd, Berkshire (1985).

Brown, P; Cox, AJ; Dumbleton, .; Noble, L; Sutherland, E **Wider Still: An Agenda for Action**, SFEU (1996).

Chapter 3
Widening participation using telematics

Jette Burford

Halton College

The reasons

A decreasing number of 16-19 year-old customers and increased competition in the sector have led many colleges to invest considerable resources in strategies for reaching new student groups. Often strategies are linked to rapid advances in telecommunication technologies. Effective exploration of new technologies will enable colleges to tap into new markets and optimise this competitive edge before the skills and technology become commonplace.

Incorporation of colleges and subsequent government-led demands for continuous cost reductions have put traditional community learning at risk. New approaches are essential to safeguard the survival and improvement of community learning initiatives. Market research and experience clearly tell us that the need for community learning is very real. Careful attention should be paid to the many telematics developments which can facilitate the learning needs of FE customers.

Leading business consultants believe that organisations must be 'bi focal' to remain successful — they must deal effectively with the demands of today while planning and preparing for the future. The Fairbairn Fellowship project at Halton College is an excellent example of bi focal vision. It meets a current local demand for access to learning opportunities while enabling the college to acquire skills and expertise in a new technology which will be used to reach new national and international student markets.

The project

Halton College serves the Cheshire towns of Widnes and Runcorn, two local communities with very different socio-economic structures. Widnes is an old town, whereas Runcorn was created during the sixties. The area is dominated by heavy manufacturing industry and has been suffering from industrial decline. Large groups of employees are excluded from FE due to shiftwork patterns; others have suffered redundancy or have been unable to find employment. Low income and low self-esteem are frequently the consequences, and they create barriers to FE. The district also has a higher than average number of single parents — approximately 7,000 — of whom most are economically inactive. A lack of affordable childcare places and an expensive and unreliable transport system add to this difficult situation.

The aim of the Fairbairn Fellowship project is to provide new access routes to FE for disadvantaged learners.

The project has specifically:

- piloted the use of desktop videoconferencing to provide learning opportunities in the community for single parents in Runcorn

- integrated computer-based multimedia into mainstream provision

Market research

In co-operation with the Responsive College Unit in Blackburn, the College conducted extensive market research. The first stage aimed to identify, locate and quantify disadvantaged groups of learners. It was decided that single parents in the Runcorn area should form the initial target group.

Using postal questionnaires and focus groups the second stage established the learning needs, suitable learning styles and support systems of the target group.

Some of the results challenged our preconceived ideas of the type of services that would interest that group. They revealed an overwhelming interest in learning at home or in the community. The subjects that generated the most enthusiasm were basic skills, IT, business studies and languages. Twenty-eight per cent of the single parents had no qualifications compared with a national average of 22%. The main reasons for wanting to participate were to find a job, to gain a qualification and to gain confidence. The research confirmed the need for social activity, interactivity and support, and established clearly that 'Open University-style' programmes are a 'complete turn-off' for this group of learners.

Community learning via videoconferencing

Assisted by additional funds from BT, Halton College built a videoconferencing network comprising the College, four schools and a library in Runcorn. Subsequently courses in Communications (pre-GCSE English), German, French and IT have been delivered via the videoconferencing network. Careers advice is also delivered on-line to student groups and the general public.

The courses have used different models designed by the individual tutors. Originally the German course was only eight weeks long, but ten of the 14 students re-enrolled on a one-year course and are now working towards a St Martins Level One Proficiency certificate. Approximately 60% of the course has been delivered via the videoconferencing. A projector and improved sound equipment have been installed at the school to allow the large group of students to see and hear the tutor clearly.

The IT students have achieved a City & Guilds 7261/212 certificate in Computers and Computing in a course delivered entirely by videoconferencing. The prerequisites for the course are software enabling the tutor and students to share computer applications and a 'drop-in' computer facility at the school.

The videoconferencing courses delivered to local schools have already assisted more than 30 students who would not otherwise have participated in a college course. Most students have achieved at least one qualification and many are progressing on to further courses. Many of the students were single parents with low incomes and very low confidence levels.

The provision on offer during autumn 1996 has been extended to include basic Maths, basic English, German, French, Italian, IT and Hair and Beauty Therapy. Soon Dressmaking and Soft Furnishing will be on offer as well.

Videoconferencing by language course students

Case studies

Sue is a student on the videoconferencing course in Communications. She is 24 years old and lives at Castlefields, Runcorn, with her six-year-old daughter. Not really interested in education, she left school in 1988 with seven GCSEs at grade D. After her daughter started school Sue had more time on her hands but didn't know how to use it. Going back to college did cross her mind, but as she says, 'I always found an excuse not to'. Sue writes 'Last year when I got a letter inviting me to join a videoconferencing course, I jumped at the idea. I knew this was possibly my only chance. I attended the first meeting at the Grange School and suddenly became very nervous. You see, the Grange was the school I left in 1988. I forced myself to carry on going to the course and it has been brilliant. I can honestly say it is the best thing I have ever done. It has boosted my confidence and made me enjoy and appreciate education.'

Sue achieved a City & Guilds certificate in Communications at stage three. She has now enrolled on a second videoconferencing course learning German, and is hoping to take an access course at Halton College next year in preparation for a university degree.

Karen is 32 years old. She also lives in Castlefields with her two children and is attending the Communications course like Sue. Unlike Sue, Karen has a car and is not prevented from attending College because of transport. Her biggest problem is childcare. The Fairbairn Project has been able to assist Karen with a small amount to help pay for childcare twice a week.

Karen writes, 'My school days were a shambles, I never attended on a regular basis. When I was at school I felt no incentive to learn. I found it hard to concentrate and the teachers found it hard to tolerate me, so it was easier to stay off school. The main thing I have learned since joining the videoconferencing course is that there is a life outside my front door. I have enjoyed going to the course, and although I have learned just basic things it makes me feel like an achiever.' Karen has achieved a City & Guilds certificate in Communications stage three and the external assessor considered her portfolio 'exceptionally good'. She is now planning to join a computing course, but is still worrying about money for childcare.

Research

Structured research applied to practical models in a real community environment provided us with unique results. It explored the support needs and the attitudes of learners to technological solutions. The information was collected from more than 100 questionnaires and interviews conducted with students, tutors and technical support staff. Statistics on retention rates and achievements have also been compared with the results from groups taught using traditional methods. The process is not complete at the time of writing but there are clear indications that the new delivery models are successful.

The research results listed below must be noted with caution, partly because the activities are not yet complete and partly because of the limited student population used. With this in mind, the information indicates that:

- there is no significant difference in retention rate between videoconferencing courses and traditional courses — no students left because of the delivery method

- students' achievements on the videoconferencing courses are equal to or higher than those of students on traditional courses

- most of the students have progressed to another videoconferencing course or a more traditional course

Feedback from students and tutors indicates that:

- students are happy to attend the local school but generally would not participate if the course was offered at the College's main site

- some students prefer to attend their videoconferencing class in the school rather than from home — mainly because there are too many distractions at home and working in a group is enjoyable

- group identity is extremely strong, probably because of the 'real-life problem-solving' the groups have to cope with

- students have perceived 'independence' from their tutor, which gives them a great confidence boost

- some students think 'it is less intimidating than a traditional lecture'

- some students feel 'special' or 'privileged' using the newest technology

- gaining qualifications is the main drive for the students to work hard

- videoconferencing tends to focus the mind — one student said 'we do more work when videoconferencing'

- basic skills tutors believe that the medium is not suitable for learning (very) basic spelling or reading

- good technical support is necessary; persistent problems have a very negative effect on staff and students

- students quickly gain the confidence to switch on and handle the equipment without assistance

- good quality sound is more important than good quality video

The great confidence boost that most students experience may be the reason that many of the students progress to further education and training. There is little doubt that using the newest technology makes students feel special, a reminder of how important it is to celebrate student and staff achievements.

A detailed report of the results will be available by the end of 1996.

Integration of multimedia on mainstream courses

'Multimedia is now part of everyday life at Halton College'

Students on most substantial programmes spend, as part of their course, a minimum of 12 hours in the College's learning centre where they plan, design and produce a multimedia learning package related to their course. The students are supported by their lecturer and a member of the multimedia team. Since the start of the Fairbairn Fellowship project more than 900 students of all ages, from a wide range of subject areas, and their lecturers have participated. The effect of the programme has resulted in staff and students realising the power of multimedia as a tool for expressing any subject. It is the benefits of this 'culture change' that make the project so attractive and well worth the investment in time and money.

Multimedia team support for students

Halton College's multimedia team produce qualification-specific packages in partnership with the subject tutors and the students. Some of these packages have been used to enhance the Fellowship project.

A Multimedia Study Skills Pack has been used at outreach centres in the community to teach basic English, Communications and general Study Skills. By the end of 1995 use by 445 students had been recorded, 169 were full-time students, 124 were in full-time employment, the rest unemployed, long-term sick, home carer or retired. More than half the students were female and more than half were more than 21 years old. A student in the 31-40 age group commented, 'Points made were accurate and relevant to the majority of mature students. The advice given to overcome the difficulties encountered when returning to College is helpful and encourages positive thinking. The programme is taken at an ideal pace — not too fast so that you miss anything, not too slow so that you get bored.'

The study skills pack has also proved to be a very effective marketing tool for enrolment of mature students in local community centres and schools on to the College's basic skills programmes.

Hairdressing multimedia packages have been used to make the programmes even more flexible than previously. Many of the students are mature women with work and family commitments. The multimedia packs make it possible for such students to study at their own pace and at a time which suits them. So far these packs have been used by over 100 students.

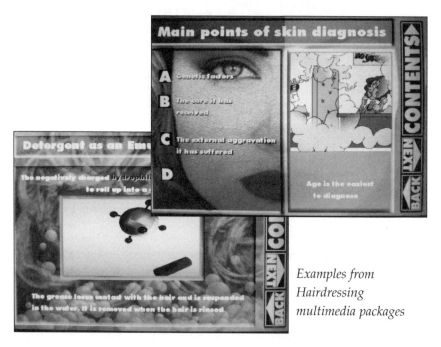

Examples from Hairdressing multimedia packages

Factors for success

Many factors contributed to the success of the project. Only the most significant are listed here:

- the project is part of the College's strategic plan and has been a catalyst for the implementation of several related strategies
- injection of funds from other sources
- ownership, responsibility and workload have been shared widely with colleagues
- time has been invested in project planning
- contingency plans were put into effect, as an external partnership arrangement did not flourish within the time span of the project period
- large-scale staff development during all phases of the project
- emphasis on embedding the new developments, followed by a conscious decision to 'let go'
- expert advice and support from the Fairbairn Fellowship Steering Group, the College Steering Group and Kevin Donovan of FEDA

Factors which should be avoided in future projects include:

- high dependence on newly established external partnerships
- external partners with plenty of enthusiasm but no budget to match it

Conclusion

The project conclusively proves that the curriculum can be developed to a format which is suitable for a telematics approach. Videoconferencing and multimedia provide access for students who would not otherwise participate. Given the right mix of support, skills and technology the delivery models are real solutions to real needs. The challenge is now to make the delivery models cost-effective. A reduction in cost of equipment and telecommunication charges is imperative. It will also be necessary to improve the study conditions in the schools and to enhance the tutors' skills further to cope with groups on two or more sites simultaneously.

Jette Burford is Head of Research and Development at Halton College.

Chapter 4
The interactive television project

Byron J. Lawson

Clarendon College, Nottingham

Background

Developing education and training opportunities to meet the needs of the twenty-first century provided the backdrop to this project. Rapid progress in the integration of data, voice and video technologies coupled with the rise of fibre optic services from newly-formed cable companies in the UK have given rise to a high level of expectation. There is increasing interest across all sectors in the development of applications to harness fibre optic technology. Considering these significant developments and the need to meet increasing demand for flexible, self-paced, self-accessed learning, we set about developing the application of telecommunications to increase participation and access to learning.

Many studies have identified reluctance, particularly in disadvantaged groups, to travel in pursuit of training. Individual studies have defined the key barriers experienced by learners as time, location, culture, environment, cost and relevance. Constructive use of videoconferencing to address these needs has opened the door for many learners, from organisations as well as individuals. The purpose of the interactive television network is to provide learning opportunities at venues accessible to all, which can be delivered irrespective of the number of participants at any one location. The ability to link centres in a fully interactive teaching session (the ability to see, hear and talk to, in real time, participants in other centres and vice versa) by using fibre optic cable links is the mechanism which makes it possible.

The interactive television network

In order to implement this ambitious project it was necessary to seek support not only from the Fairbairn Fellowship but from a number of external organisations. The result is a partnership with the primary purpose of building economic and social improvement for the population between:

- Clarendon College Nottingham Corporation

- Nottingham City Council
- Greater Nottingham Training Enterprise Council
- Nottingham City Challenge
- The Nottingham Trent University
- Diamond Cable Communications
- GPT-Communication Systems Limited

These organisations have made a significant investment and the money is enhanced by their donation of time, expertise and substantial networking opportunities. The college would like to take this opportunity to thank all the above organisations for their continued enthusiasm and support.

The aims of this work are to increase significantly participation by under-represented groups in FE and to develop effective teaching and learning styles. The initial research work identified the skills needed to support a staff development programme. These specific aims are complemented by the opportunity to broaden and enhance the curriculum for existing school and FE students. From a macro-perspective they mirror the corporate aims of widening access and participation, investing in development of our staff and improvement of our systems and resources.

Aims

- to increase participation rates in education and training, particularly by disadvantaged groups, through the lowering of traditional barriers such as time, mobility and culture
- to provide participants with access to new technologies
- to develop teaching and learning strategies to support interactive learning opportunities
- to share good practice

Objectives

- to establish a 'network' of interactive training venues in the inner city

- to increase participation significantly by the unemployed, ethnic minorities, women returners and people with disabilities

- to provide opportunities which support intercultural activities in a multicultural society

- to investigate and evaluate delivery mechanisms and processes

- to identify and share examples of good practice

- to integrate the use of interactive technologies within the curriculum portfolio

Clarendon College interactive TV: students using the videoconferencing system to improve access to education and training at the local community centre

creating connections

The network

The network features the following locations across the inner city:

Venue	Location
Clarendon College main site	Forest Fields/Mapperley
Clarendon College King Street	City Centre
Nottingham Trent University Business School	City Centre
African Caribbean Women's Project	St Ann's District
Greenwood Junior School	Sneinton District

Centres were selected on their experience, ability and past record in working with communities targeted in this project including:

- women returners

- the unemployed

- ethnic minorities

- people with disabilities

- carers

Each centre has a room with videoconferencing equipment providing access for up to 12 people. It is possible through linking all these centres to provide access to up to 60 users or, more importantly, the ability to meet the demand made by as few as two or three per centre. Centres are linked with a high bandwidth fibre optic connection to Clarendon's main site which holds the multipoint control unit. This provides access for all centres to the national and international telephone networks.

Whatever the situation, one teacher is able to communicate effectively with all participants; the teacher can select at which centre they wish to be present in person. The technology also allows the distribution of data, graphics and video; participants are able to gain access to all the learning resources that would be available at the main site. These resources have been increased to include access to the Internet. If paper-based materials are required for a session, they are distributed before the scheduled start but can also be sent by fax.

Centres also provide créche and childcare support for participants; close work with 'Fast Forward' (the government-funded initiative to develop inner-city training, especially for women returners) has identified more support needs.

The environment

In order to reach those target groups for whom provision and services require development or modification the following, particularly significant, external factors need to be addressed:

- a predicted post-recession shortage in IT, language and supervisory skills

- recognising that non-manual occupations are demanding more product knowledge, communication skills, keyboard skills and wider commercial awareness

- high level of unemployment in the inner city compared to both county and national statistics

- the change of the employment base away from manufacturing towards service industries

- of the recognised area population 42% have no formal qualifications; 64% of people with adult basic education (ABE) needs have never attended classes

- 3,824 in the City Challenge area were identified as having limiting long-term illness

The Interactive Television Network uses state-of-the-art technology to extend the education and training opportunities available to inner-city disadvantaged communities. Dial-up services have also been installed to increase the scope of the network. Centres can now access locations throughout the world through Integrated Services Digital Network

(ISDN) which offers users the opportunity to experience, share and learn from other regions and countries.

Progress in the installation of the network was much delayed while awaiting the outcome of an unsuccessful European Regional Development Fund bid. The initial project (an eight-centre network) then had to be redrafted and support from partners reaffirmed. This was unanimous and the installation of the present five-centre network was completed in November 1995. Installation and purchase costs were met entirely by the partners.

A number of successful programmes have been delivered across a range of centres with up to ten hours per week of programmes available between March and May (see Figure 4.1 on page 48).

Where are we now?

Planning for this year (1996-7) identifies a weekly output of 20 hours. A wide range of student groups, community organisations, local schools and FE colleges from regions throughout the country have been involved. Links with many of these organisations are being developed in anticipation of forthcoming collaboration. For example, a school on the outskirts of the city has purchased their own videoconferencing equipment following demonstrations and involvement in sessions, with a view to supporting GNVQ and progression for their pupils with the assistance of the college.

Recruitment to date has been affected by the delays in establishing the network but its adoption by curriculum directors as a mechanism for extending markets, identifying new programmes and providing flexible access to existing programmes is evidence of positive views. For example, Art and Design have scheduled an art appreciation programme which reflects the cultural variation of the network centres (both Afro-Caribbean and Asian) and includes contributions by American and Canadian artists via videoconferencing.

Figure 4.1
Activity January to May 1995-6

Programme delivery	Number of participants	Total hours
Curriculum *A- level Communication Studies* *GNVQ Business & Finance* *NVQ Level 2 Administration & Assertiveness*	96	84
Staff development	41	32
Promotional events, community, education & industry	117	74

One important feature has been the level of interest shown by lecturing staff; 41 people have received initial training across a wide range of curriculum areas:

Hair & Beauty Business & Management Studies
Floristry Community Education
Languages IT & Administration
Leisure Catering & Hospitality Management

A user's guide was produced after initial trial programmes over a point-to-point link using existing students, and a detailed evaluation of both teacher and student response. This work provides a very good base on which to develop multipoint techniques; teachers need to be aware of people in multiple centres and to use specific question and response tactics to maintain involvement by all participants. Video and CD-ROM versions of this guide will be available shortly.

Comments from staff (and students) include 'I don't like seeing myself on screen' and 'it is akin to fronting a TV chat show without the cosy settee ... the reality horror is that you are fronting a TV chat show — without the show and without the dress allowance'.

One curriculum director commented after the first 20 minutes of her first session (no previous experience), 'they all want to be on screen ... in fact the ladies said that they would get their hair done for next week', and these were on an assertiveness course.

Initial staff responses have now changed to 'the network provides an opportunity to experience a realistic context in which to test the skills required to keep abreast of new technologies', 'I definitely need to update my skills in presentation and assembling materials' and 'this will provide my students with realistic experience of what the world of work will have to offer in the very near future'.

The experiences reported here have contributed to an increased demand for IT skills initial training for some staff and updating and skilling for others. The network has contributed significantly to increased awareness of technology and its benefit for education.

It is difficult to attribute specific learning benefits for individual students using this medium; the previous recorded level of ability has no direct correlation with who 'performs' well. It was clear though that students found this an 'exciting learning environment'. This, we felt, was initially a reflection of technology rather than content but they were soon noticing that 'the scope for development was immense' and that this was a relaxing environment once initial 'phobias' were overcome. A-level Communications students chose to deliver their final oral examination over the network for assessment; they also insisted on creating computer -based presentations to support their talk.

Some students, who had been reluctant to contribute to classroom discussion found a new confidence whereas others, a music student used to public recitals for example, did not respond happily or willingly.

This was apparent across several 16-19 groups where peer-group pressure was far more evident.

Adult users, however, were a different proposition; within ten minutes of their first encounter with the technology they were relishing the opportunity to exploit it, recognising the benefits:

'I only live up the road from ACNA*, it would be easier for me to get there.'
* the African Caribbean National Association (the centre is in the women's project)

'If I could afford a computer I could stay at home.'

Their ability to recognise the benefits of this technology is evidence to support our ambition of providing links into individual homes.

Peter, an adult returner with a physical disability found access to King Street far more attractive than the main site but the programme had not previously been available there.

Dora and June didn't know that Clarendon offered courses in Floristry. A visit to ACNA enabled them to join a floristry taster course delivered from the main site; they will be enrolling in September.

Evidence will soon be available to support the achievement of recruitment targets following extensive taster and promotional activities. This first phase has provided valuable guidance and opportunities to integrate the technology with the curriculum portfolio and corporate developments.

The success of this project has been one of the factors contributing to the development of an 'electronic campus strategy' — a phased implementation of technologies to meet the needs of the lifelong learner. The extension of the use of videoconferencing is a major feature of this strategy.

Where next?

The initial project has been extended to support training in the workplace via videoconferencing and is going well. There are opportunities here for closer links between education and industry, and for students to gain direct insights into commercial organisations. It also provides a direction for training opportunities in the home. Delivery of training via interactive services will soon be possible without a computer as cable companies, in particular, progress with enabling the 'set top box' (the decoder/encoder box with satellite TV) to receive and transmit computer data.

The ability to provide remote, dial-up access to tutors, self-paced learning materials on CD-ROM, enrolment and guidance services will enable the college to provide a service to meet the lifelong learning needs of the community. We plan to extend the partnership to include centres from across the East Midlands, to offer opportunities for skills exchange between colleges, extend the range of curriculum available and provide access to the work environment. These advances will all be focused on disadvantaged learners; the network will provide access to new skills in areas of industrial decline without the need to travel.

The MORI State of the Nation poll into attitudes to education and training in May of this year states that 95% of respondents believe in lifetime learning but:

> If learning is to compete in the high street it will have to be packaged as a desirable product and be innovatively branded in a way which infiltrates people's lifestyles. Once interest is created, opportunities will need to be accessed as quickly and easily as any other lifestyle product on display.

> Tamsin Butters, Speaker at MORI, State of Nations Conference

Innovative use of new technologies is a key factor in that packaging.

Byron Lawson is the Interactive Multimedia Services Manager at Clarendon College, Nottingham.

Chapter 5

Managing key skills: a multimedia staff development package

Paul O'Doherty

Western Education and Library Board
Northern Ireland

In the beginning

Although the last to begin, Northern Ireland was delighted to host a Fairbairn project. Colleges submitted a wide variety of project proposals all of which used new technology. One topic in particular caught the attention of the steering group — core (now key) skills. A survey by the Inspectorate had identified core/key skills as a major issue in the introduction of General National Vocational Qualifications (GNVQs). At first it seemed that the technology might be used directly in the delivery of these skills but gradually a different model of empowerment began to emerge. This proposed that students could best benefit when staff themselves became empowered both to master these skills and the new technology itself. After much discussion it was agreed to produce a staff development package for college staff. This achievement of consensus on the aim of the project and its associated objectives was the first crucial step in the formation of a very creative partnership.

Partners

It was this partnership that was to become the most distinctive aspect of the Northern Ireland project. No one college owns the project. Instead it is a collaboration between a variety of educational bodies. The Department of Education in Northern Ireland and the Regional Training Unit agreed to match funds with the Esmée Fairbairn Charitable Trust. Additional resources were provided by the Education and Library Boards (there are five regional authorities which jointly manage a regional training unit). The Northern Ireland Centre for Learning Resources (NICLR) co-ordinated the CD-ROM design and scripting, developed the software and filmed the video material. Finally all 17 colleges in Northern Ireland provided experience of and insight into delivering key skills: application of number, communication, IT, working with others, improving own learning and performance and problem solving.

All these skills were to be demonstrated by those involved in the project. Perhaps the most important skill proved to be working with teams of talented people and gaining their co-operation and consensus. The steering committee included representatives from the Association for Colleges (now the Association of Colleges), the Department of Education, NICLR, the Education and Library Boards and principals of colleges. It maintained an overview of the project development, budgets and liaison with the other Fairbairn projects. The next team was a core working party that advised on and developed the fundamental structures. This team met at least once a month and was the driving engine of the project. It was augmented by college staff seconded to the project to develop particular aspects of the material.

Work was also carried out very effectively in residentials where staff with specialist expertise (including principals, heads of department, course co-ordinators and key skills tutors) could contribute to the

Script writing workshop

development of scripts and modules free from the distractions of the normal working environments. All of these experiences helped secure a better understanding of what we needed to achieve as well as a great appreciation of the creativity and commitment of those who contributed.

In between these activities, the NICLR team quietly steered us through the intricacies of developing a multimedia package. Between residentials and group meetings we would sift through the material, edit the scripts and slowly evolve our initial concepts. We used scripts developed by the actual practitioners and filmed in a variety of college locations using college staff wherever possible. Slowly we developed modules for the package. As we approached the end of the project we nervously considered whether the package was coherent and consistent and if it achieved our primary objective — to aid staff delivery of key

Figure 5.1: Managing key skills — content grid

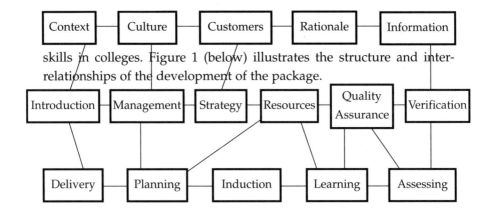

skills in colleges. Figure 1 (below) illustrates the structure and inter-relationships of the development of the package.

In the end

The outcome of all these endeavours is a CD-ROM for college staff ranging from vocational and key skills tutors to senior management. The structure of the programme allows staff complete freedom to work in any topic (or module) area that they select. For ease of use these modules are grouped in three sets:

- context
- management
- delivery

All the modules in the **context** set explore the culture and ethos surrounding key skills delivery. For instance, there is a module on the rationale for the introduction of these skills expressed from a variety of perspectives: college principal, industry, NCVQ and awarding bodies. The next set of modules is aimed at the **management** of the skills in college. Again a variety of staff may benefit from using them, e.g. course co-ordinators may wish to consider aspects of quality assurance and senior management may wish to delve into strategic considerations. An underlying assumption in all this was that staff at all levels might gain better understanding of each other's role and contribution by having access to all modules. The final set contains the bulk of the material and is intended to assist staff (both vocational and key skills tutors) directly in the **delivery** of key skills. It does not prescribe any one model but through a variety of exercises invites teams and individuals to explore how their own college might meet the challenge of key skills delivery.

The package has been designed for use both by individuals and by groups. The exercises can be done individually but often are most useful as a stimulus for group discussion. Individuals or teams can log on with their own password allowing them to maintain confidentiality and their own particular perspective. The intention is to evolve mutual understanding of the issues and circumstances in which the team operates, then to allow the group to determine strategies for improving performance.

This approach envisages a crucial role for a group leader or facilitator who may be course co-ordinator, staff development tutor or a skilled team member. The package has proved most useful when the tutor uses insight about the college and experience of the way the team operates. The CD-ROM is a valuable tool but its effectiveness depends on the person using it. An initial copy of the completed disk will be sent to all the Northern Ireland colleges.

The final but vital stage of any project is dissemination. Since this project started from scratch most of the initial energy went into planning and developing the curricular material itself. Feedback mechanisms were built into the various parts as the project developed. The core team is now working with a variety of college teams to make a comprehensive evaluation of the project.

Looking back

Reflecting on the development of this project it is possible to learn some lessons which are transferable to a wide range of activities. The major areas are:

- dealing with change
- working with people
- managing resources

Dealing with change

As the project developed there were some significant changes. The revision of the National Targets for Education and Training (NETTs) with their specific reference to core skills raised the profile of the whole issue for an ever wider range of bodies. The high profile of core skills in non-GNVQ programmes also meant that the material needed a wider set of exemplars to be applicable to practically every course in a college. The content and layout of the core skills were themselves revised.

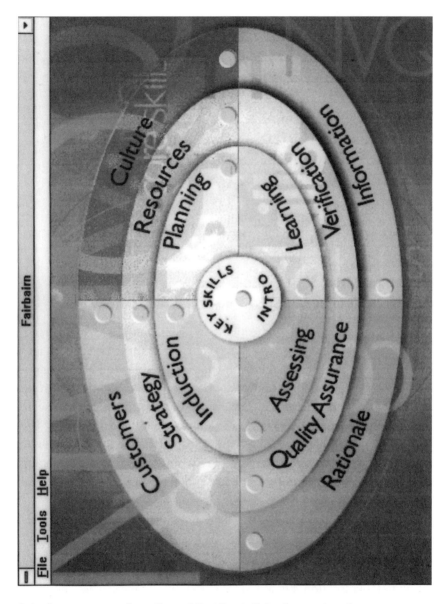

Introductory screen from the multimedia staff development package

There were also many major reviews during this period with implications for project content. Clearly the most significant was the Dearing Review of 16-19 which led among other things to a change in terminology from core skills to key skills.

The conclusion is that if a topical project is to have long-term usefulness, the project team must anticipate developments, address underlying themes and concepts which are less susceptible to change and ensure maximum flexibility in the material itself.

Working with people

Most activities involve people: people to whom you are accountable, people you must co-operate with and people to lead or inform. By the nature of human existence these are likely to change over the years. In the course of this project, career progression has meant that key team members left and a new team had to be built.

Introducing new members or bringing in people temporarily has meant a large investment of time and energy. Both experienced and inexperienced members had to be made comfortable with each other. It was necessary to define and redefine the objectives of the group continuously. Individuals were encouraged to contribute, to criticise, to explore new avenues but in the end to reach a consensus. The combination of residentials with a core group of people working over an extended time was an extremely useful mechanism for developing coherence within diversity. Of course it helps to have gifted and committed team members.

Managing resources

Any project has to work within a budget, but it is also important not to let initial exploration be too dominated by finance. The, 'how' of implementation is much more flexible than is often credited. In this project the team was encouraged to explore all possibilities suggested in a wide variety of approaches. Often these were later curtailed not

Multimedia development team at work

because of finance but because of other considerations. For instance, teaching staff were used rather than professional actors, because of their familiarity and ease with the language and concepts. Similarly each module initially used different approaches to help achieve a freshness and novelty but this was eventually modified in order to help the user have a sense of familiarity with the system. Thus certain tools are present in a number of modules and similar exercises are used in different modules to help teams reflect points made.

The greatest resource has been the generosity of those involved. The additional funding from the Department of Education and the Education and Library Boards are concrete facts. More intangible but of more value has been the generosity of time, energy and creativity of the people involved. This is the key resource on which any project depends.

Our target audience in Northern Ireland is the staff of the 17 FE colleges. This totals approximately 2,200 staff of whom 100 were directly involved. We hope that their experiences will cascade to the rest. The range of courses supported ran the full gamut from Advanced GNVQs in Business Studies to courses in carpentry. And the most important lesson? Collaboration is vital to provide quality provision of the curriculum.

Paul O'Doherty is Adviser for Vocational Education and Careers at the Western Education and Library Board, based in Omagh, County Tyrone.

Chapter 6
On-line with Europe/Open learning for delivery of foreign languages and EFL

Danny Price and Judy Hargreaves

South Kent College

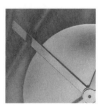

Introduction

In making the bid for Fairbairn funding two related projects were envisaged at South Kent College. First, we wanted to develop on-line links with existing and new partner institutions in other European countries as a support for training in modern languages.

Secondly, we wanted to develop open learning programmes for the delivery and support of foreign language and English as a Foreign Language (EFL) courses.

The on-line project was assigned to Danny Price, a lecturer in French and English as a Foreign Language in the European Business and Language Centre, with experience of language course writing for corporate clients and many years' experience of international telecommunications with British Telecom.

Open learning programmes are being developed by Judy Hargreaves, Manager of the European Business and Language Centre, who is responsible for the delivery of language courses across the college and to corporate clients.

On-line with Europe

Over the years South Kent College has worked with partner colleges and training institutions in France, Germany, Holland and Denmark. Collaboration across the curriculum has consisted of students spending short periods of work experience abroad, working alongside their European partners in the foreign college or taking part in educational and cultural visits.

New technology offers the possibility of enhanced contact, enriching traditional links by enabling students here and in our partner colleges to collaborate in a more continuous way. Fairbairn support has enabled us to look at doing this by using on-line technology, notably audio-conferencing and e-mail.

Audio conferencing

Voice communication has an obvious role to play in language learning but an ordinary telephone is not much good between groups of students all trying to talk at once. Devices are now on the market — and becoming more affordable — that enable two or more groups of people linked via telephone lines to talk to each other. This is an audio-conference.

In June 1994 I visited the Lycée Romain Rolland in Amiens, one of our partners for several years, to discuss collaboration through the use of on-line technology. They were already conducting trials of audio- and videoconferencing with a college in the north of England and were keen to develop further their link with our Business Studies students in Ashford. It seemed to us that audioconferencing could be a valuable tool for language training and we decided to carry out a trial later that month when tutors from Amiens would be visiting Ashford. As we didn't yet have the equipment I borrowed it from BT.

The device is called an AC4600 and consists of three microphones mounted around a central loudspeaker. Like an ordinary telephone it has a keypad for dialling and is connected to an ordinary telephone line. The French were using more sophisticated equipment (paid for by funding from their region) connected to Numéris, the France Télécom equivalent of BT's ISDN2. We could not dial them, presumably because they were connected to Numéris and not to the ordinary telephone system, but they could call us and soon we at Ashford were talking to the group at Amiens. Speaking within about a metre of the nearest microphone the sound quality and audibility were very satisfactory. A group of six can talk easily with a similar group at the other end. We discussed how to write a c.v. in French and in English, comparing the differences in format and content.

The purpose of the trial was to examine how learners of French in Ashford and learners of English in Amiens could speak to each other on a prepared topic. Doing it this way would enable learners to research their topic, learn vocabulary and practise before going on line and speaking French or English for real. We considered this would help to build confidence at speaking a foreign language to native speakers and, because the topics form part of their other business studies, would be directly relevant to them. It would also help to build confidence to take part in exchanges and work placements abroad.

e-mail

We have been using BT's Campus 2000, recently replaced by Campus World, an on-line service for schools and colleges. I was particularly interested in getting tutors and students to use e-mail with partners abroad as a means both of practising use of a foreign language and of collaborating on joint projects related to their course. e-mail, by enabling them to practise writing and reading skills, would complement audio-conferencing, which enhances speaking and listening skills.

Finding partners willing to try new technology

I was lucky in finding partners in the Lycée Romain Rolland already equipped and ready to use audioconferencing. Unfortunately so far they have not tried e-mail. Another lycée in Douai audio-conferences with us using an ordinary telephone. This means that only one French student at a time can talk to our students, but they do now have access to a server, a recent acquisition which is enabling us to exchange e-mail and data files, and which will be ready for use from September 1996.

Working with a foreign college

To exploit on-line technology to the full, several factors have to be considered. Student groups need to be identified and matched as closely as possible for linguistic ability, course syllabus, and vocational and linguistic objectives.

For example, in planning the collaboration with the Lycée Corot in Douai, the French and English tutors exchanged course programmes for the groups of students in mind: business administration students at South Kent College and tri-lingual secretaries in Douai. This enabled common areas of learning to be identified.

The French and English tutors met to iron out practical details such as ensuring that both groups of students attended their language classes at the same time, important for audioconferencing but not at all for e-mail. Topics for audioconferencing were decided and a timetable drawn up. Personal details of students were exchanged and an exchange visit to each other's college planned.

Ashford students and tutor audio-conferencing with students in Amiens

Audio conferencing on prepared topics

French and English students prepare a topic with their own tutor over two or three weeks. They then go on-line to talk to each other using the prepared topic as a guide. In order to practise both listening and speaking skills, the first half of each session is conducted in French and the second half in English or vice versa.

e-mail will also be used from September 1996 to send information, questions, etc. to the other group to help each other prepare for the on-line sessions.

Student and tutor reaction

This has been very positive and is bearing fruit; at the time of writing one of our adult evening classes has heard of it and wants to try it. I have found a similar group for them in France and they will shortly be speaking to each other on line.

What some of our students think about audio-conferencing:

'It gave us direct experience, i.e. improving our French by speaking to native speakers and it gave us confidence as we heard how they were at English.'

'I got to practise my French in a real-life environment and it made a change from lessons.'

'(The link-ups) were very interesting; it allowed the class to use their knowledge of the language to their full extent.'

'It was good to talk to people in another country; it is a good way to learn French.'

Going on-line gives students the benefit of direct contact with native speakers. More and more students will start to see learning a language as a meaningful and enjoyable experience that can be of great use to them both at work and at leisure.

Conclusion

To date 30 students at South Kent College and 35 at three colleges in Northern France have taken part in audio-conferencing links as an integral part of French and English language training programmes. These numbers are set to grow.

The on-line project has been partly about finding partners willing to try out new technology. One of our newest links — with Västerviks Gymnasium in Sweden is now beginning to take off with Media Studies students here and in Sweden working on a joint project. Another project with Västerviks will link our two colleges with one in Portugal, initially for a programme of teacher exchanges. Plumbing students at South Kent college will be linking with plumbing students at the Lycée Normandie Niemen in Calais during the next college year. Such links are extending beyond the narrow field of language training and will therefore affect larger numbers of students.

The road to open learning

At the start of the project the idea was to set up an open learning centre with a multimedia computer in the language lab on each college site (Dover, Folkestone and Ashford). However, this soon proved impractical because of accessibility, security, staffing, and conflict of use with classes — not to mention a lack of open learning students.

CD-ROM for language learning

It was then decided to look at the availability of CD-ROMs and evaluate existing material. There was not much available at the time (1994) and what there was seemed poor value for money in terms of effective language learning — most textbooks were deemed more useful and far cheaper!

Over the three years of the project we have continued to evaluate CD-ROM resources and are pleased to report that the last two years have seen a wealth of material streaming on to the market, particularly in the four main European languages — French, German, Spanish and Italian. Some are even designed to meet the assessment criteria of NVQ programmes! Costs, however, are still high, especially with material at an intermediate or advanced level.

Language workshops

We decided to run a French language workshop for two hours each week making use of a room in the library area at two college sites early on in the 1995-6 academic year, as a forerunner to developing an open learning facility. The workshops were only available to full-time students seeking additional learning support. They were run initially to suit staff availability rather than student timetables and were not well attended, but attendance improved considerably when the workshops were re-scheduled to times requested by the students. Students were taught individually or in small groups of three or four with a wide range of resources available — textbooks, cassettes, videos and CD-ROMs. A French language specialist was always available throughout the workshop to ensure effective monitoring of the activity. It was noted that A-level students in particular made use of this facility.

The new open learning centre at Dover

In September 1996 the first of the college's open learning centres will be operational. This will be located on the entire second floor of an existing teaching block, replacing six classrooms and linked to the library on the first floor below. When it is open we anticipate that we will attract open learners from the general public in substantial numbers, bearing in mind that many workers in this area (e.g. from the ferry companies) need French language training in particular and work irregular shift patterns making it impossible to attend traditional weekly classes.

Open learning language materials

Initially we plan to offer the four main European languages at beginner level, offering a choice of a general or business course, and in addition GCSE French or German. The main decision has been whether to make use of material already available (such as from the National Consortium), to buy in, or to produce our own. The latter is clearly the most expensive.

We have produced our own learning pack for French at beginner level working from the coursebook *French for Starters* and accompanying cassettes, and it has proved popular with a wide range of learners — from housewives to corporate clients. For other languages we are currently looking at coursebooks which are accompanied not only by cassettes of a very high quality covering a substantial amount of the content, but also by a workbook with exercises suitable for self-study.

As we evaluate the CD-ROMs, we plan to catalogue in detail their suitability for inclusion in existing language programmes, both in the classroom and also for self-study in the open learning centre.

Conclusion

The drop-in language workshops we piloted for three months at Dover and Ashford attracted 20 students on French GCSE and A-level courses. The new learning centre being set up at Dover will use the new language learning techniques developed. Other learning centres are planned for Folkestone and Ashford.

Danny Price is a lecturer and Judy Hargreaves is the Language Co-ordinator at South Kent College.

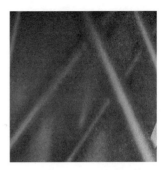

Chapter 7
Flexible science: making science more accessible

Alison Roberts

Shrewsbury College of Arts and Technology

Introduction

Shrewsbury College of Arts and Technology, with the aid of the Fairbairn Fellowship, has developed a science centre designed to improve access to science for a wide range of students who have traditionally been disadvantaged.

Science today has an image problem: many see it as poorly paid, with a limited career structure and, worst of all, endless ethical dilemmas. Science departments in colleges are therefore faced with a doubly difficult task. Not only do they need to advertise their wares in an increasingly competitive world but they also have to convince potential students that science has a future.

The gradually falling numbers of students choosing science has meant that many departments have become uneconomical and the staff have had to either diversify or adopt new, and often difficult, strategies to maintain their student groups. Although many scientists have risen to the challenge with enthusiasm and some excellent science learning experiences exist nationwide, overall morale is not high enough to compensate for the low esteem in which such work seems to be held.

What science education badly needs is a fresh, new style. What it does not need is the old one diluted.

Creating the science centre

Shrewsbury College of Arts and Technology is a typical example of the situation, with falling numbers of science students and enthusiastic staff with genuine motivation but a growing degree of despondency. The receipt of a Fairbairn Fellowship enabled the staff to spend time reviewing the perceived problems and looking at possible solutions. One member of the science team became the Fairbairn Fellow and was given the time to pursue the strategies decided on by the team. This single advantage, of time for one person to devote to the development of the initial ideas, is what drove the project forward.

The funding put forward by the college itself, to match the input from the Esmée Fairbairn Charitable Trust, was devoted to the project's first major plan, the creation of a purpose-built science centre. It was a relatively small-scale development — a single large traditional laboratory space was converted to 'state of the art'. The thinking behind this was to ensure that student perceptions of science would be altered from the first moment they encountered it. Time was spent on design and inception to ensure that it was exactly what the staff envisaged. Professional designers were only consulted once the concept had been agreed by the future users. This approach ensured that staff felt ownership of the project and an incentive to make it work.

The development of the science centre was carried out in parallel to the production of practical materials aimed particularly at students unlikely to have good access to class practicals. The emphasis was on producing a template with which the staff and students would become familiar through use: the materials were in a 'user-friendly' format to enable students to work largely independently so their confidence could grow.

Science teachers will recognise the limitations of such an approach and appreciate that the staffing of the Science Centre by a rota of competent subject staff is an essential component.

Tracking and monitoring student use of the science centre and the practical schedules available were crucial and proved to be some of the more difficult aspects of the project. In the first year the paper-based recording system very quickly proved inefficient and open to abuse. It did however indicate what records were essential and what was superfluous, so that when a computer-based system was developed there was a specific brief. The system was tailored to the needs of the science centre but its principles are adaptable. The continuing drawback is that the system is still stand-alone because the college does not currently have an operational computerised student tracking system. It is likely that when this does come on-stream the science centre system will become redundant but in the meantime it provides rapid access to information on students and the use of the science centre.

Figure 7.1: Plan of Science Centre

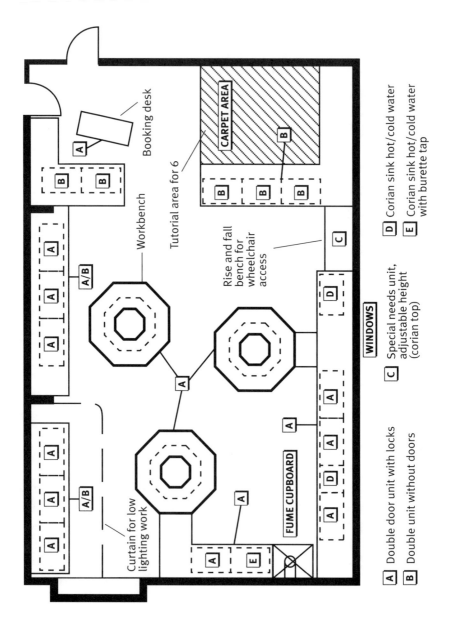

Booking desk

CARPET AREA

Workbench

Tutorial area for 6

Rise and fall bench for wheelchair access

WINDOWS

A/B

A/B

FUME CUPBOARD

Curtain for low lighting work

C Special needs unit, adjustable height (corian top)

D Corian sink hot/cold water

E Corian sink hot/cold water with burette tap

A Double door unit with locks

B Double unit without doors

Benefits of the project

The students who have benefited most from the project so far are undoubtedly those with least usual access — open learning and other part-time students especially, but also those who have missed classes or failed to complete an assignment in the usual class time. There could not have been a GNVQ science group without the science centre as the numbers could not justify full timetabling in the conventional framework.

Students studying by distance learning packs have needed to come into college to fulfil the practical elements of their courses and it has been possible for them to arrange these sessions to fit in with their own circumstances. These circumstances have included part- or full-time work, childcare and school runs. There were four students taking GCSE Human Physiology and Health and three students taking A-level Environmental Science this year for whom the science centre was the enabling factor.

Case study

Wendy is an open learning student, a mother with two children of school age. She wishes to enter nursing in the future and therefore needs to pick up some further GCSEs, including a science subject. She has chosen to take the Human Physiology and Health syllabus which is designed for adult students. However, due to the demands of the Schools Curriculum Assessment Authority (SCAA) it is necessary for her to undertake assessed practical work as an integral part of the course. Since she is studying independently with the minimum of tutor time this requirement could prove very difficult.

The Science Centre provided a facility which Wendy, and other open learning students could access at their own convenience in order to obtain the necessary assessment record. Communicating by telephone Wendy was able to arrange times when she, and another OL student, could come in and work under the supervision of a suitable member of the teaching staff. This was done at times when other, more conventional, students were also in the science centre.

Wendy commented that working in the centre was very much like working in an open plan office and this made her feel much more comfortable. She did not find the presence of other students and in some cases other staff, at all distracting. The atmosphere of quiet involvement provided a positive motivation. During her first visit she was naturally rather anxious but subsequently she felt fully at ease with the environment.

The tutor was able to access pre-prepared materials in the Centre, designed for use with GCSE students and with the assessment element built in. This meant that the tutor did not need to prepare specially for her visits and therefore did not spend an unacceptable amount of time on a single student. The materials used were however appropriate for Wendy and indeed on the later visits she was able to get on with very little individual attention.

Note: Wendy gained a grade C in her GCSE and has been awarded a nursing place.

There have been other spin-offs to the original project: for example, the development of science courses for students with learning difficulties. A group of ten students with learning difficulties and disabilities were enabled to have practical science sessions — in some cases for the first time. The design of the centre is such that they and their carers were able to work with confidence under the eye of an experienced science teacher. A group of 12 students with mild learning difficulties were also able to develop practical skills in the centre. Materials have been developed with their needs in mind. This work is being expanded to two more groups in the current academic year.

Obviously the centre has been well used by the more traditional full-time students as it provides easy access to a range of facilities such as science videos, specialist computer software, data logging equipment and microscopes as well as the usual laboratory materials. There has been occasional use of the Centre and its facilities by other users such as maths students doing practical work and media students making videos.

The whole concept of learning science through self-managed programmes with the student accessing practical elements of the course as and when they feel ready, requires a complete change in outlook by both staff and students. This new culture of 'learning on demand' has a great future and could be an important part of the resurrection of science. It is in the interests of all educationalists who wish science to have a future to look at ways of advancing 'flexible science' in the FE domain.

The future of low-demand courses and subjects probably rests with facilities such as the one developed at Shrewsbury College of Arts and Technology. Certainly in areas with limited access to the whole range of

Catering for individual students by flexible programming

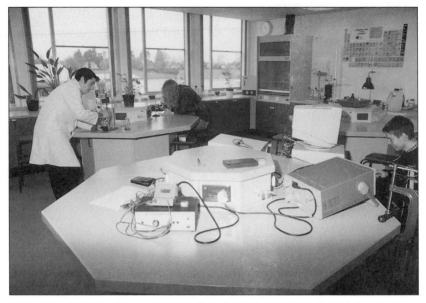

Accessing 'hands on' experience in the safety of a staffed science laboratory

educational provision, because of cost or distance or both, flexible access centres are essential. Regardless of the flowering of multimedia approaches to distance learning, science students still need to access 'hands-on' experience and this must be in the safety and comfort of managed and staffed laboratories. The extent to which the science centre can be useful is limited only by its size and the need for health and safety provision. It will doubtless grow as a wider range of users is identified.

The Fairbairn project has raised awareness of some of these issues, through the links which have been made between interested staff in different colleges and, on a broader base, through the collaboration of the Fairbairn Fellow and the Association for Science Education (ASE). This latter has resulted in a workshop session and follow-up publication in *Post-Sixteen Science Issues*, a journal of the ASE and a wider forum for addressing such matters nationally with science staff in colleges and schools.

Conclusion

It would be unreasonable to conclude without pointing out some of the major issues which must be addressed when considering any further work in this area. This cannot be a comprehensive list simply because every institution is unique, but perhaps it will provide a starting point for future development work:

- identify likely future trends — student numbers, subject choices, academic potential, spending potential

- review present facilities, their present use and their potential

- determine what programmes will meet the needs of the future market

- find out how the same problems are being addressed elsewhere — networking with other colleges will provide lots of ideas

- make sure that all the changes you plan can be built into your natural cycle of curriculum development. It is no good expecting staff to drop everything and redesign their whole teaching style over the summer holidays. Evolution is better than revolution!

- assess the long-term cost effectiveness of the changes you plan, but do not forget to build in short-term costs, even photocopying of materials soon adds up

- all of the new innovations which you introduce must be user-friendly from day one or potentially excellent schemes will fall flat on their face as students become disillusioned by early difficulties

- make sure that all the staff feel personally involved at all stages. The teaching staff and the technicians will be the ones who make any initiative work. Presenting them with *faits accompli*s in the form of a new science centre designed by an 'expert' or a set of learning materials bought for a good price may not be the best approach — unless of course it is their idea

Finally, and most importantly, keep talking — to each other, to the students, to your network of contacts.

Alison Roberts is the Area Leader for Science at Shrewsbury College of Arts and Technology.

creating connections

Chapter 8
Improving local participation through a flexible curriculum framework

Trisha Jordan and Alison Shipton

South Bristol College (now City of Bristol College)

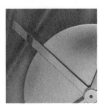

Introduction

South Bristol is an area of high unemployment and low post-16 education participation. The local population sees little benefit in education as a means to improve their prospects. The project aimed to reduce the barriers to participation and raise awareness of the benefits of education in helping to enhance the quality of life and job prospects.

It is the role of FE to give people who missed out the first time, another chance to lead a richer, more enjoyable life over which they have more control. The key is access to education in colleges and in the community to meet the aspiration to 'lifelong learning'. To make this opportunity attractive to all, it needs to be offered in a welcoming, friendly environment, in an accessible place, at a convenient time. It needs to offer understandable, relevant, flexible, accredited qualifications which recognise the wide variety of possible levels and types of learning achievements.

The project

Two staff on a job share implemented the project. Alison Shipton concentrated on research and links with local community groups and Trisha Jordan on the development of a flexible curriculum framework.

Research

This study asked why only a comparatively few local people take advantage of the learning opportunities offered in the college.

The research included a literature search, statistical review and one-to-one semi-structured interviews, a method that is considered to be most revealing of the interviewees' experiences and opinions. A range of viewpoints provided as broad a picture as possible in the time available. The interviews targeted four groups:

- South Bristol College staff

- local community services, agencies and organisations
- college participants
- local non-participants

The two questions which stimulated particularly useful responses during the interviews were:

- What do you consider to be the barriers to participation on courses at the college?
- What do you think the college could do to improve the situation ?

The project identified three types of barrier: societal, personal and institutional. As the college can only reduce the perceived institutional barriers, the project focused on these. Figure 8.1 (see page 86) summarises the research findings and includes a more detailed analysis of the institutional barriers and the college's responses.

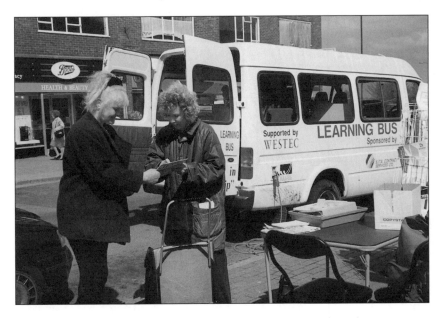

Learning Bus in Hartcliffe shopping centre, Bristol

creating connections

Figure 8.1: Barriers to Participation in South Bristol

Societal
- Lethargy of long-term unemployed
- Drugs
- Crime
- Unsafe reputation of geographical area of college

Personal
- Poor school experience
- Lack of confidence
- Loneliness and isolation

Perceived Barriers	Institutional	South Bristol College Response
Lack of community-based learning; Too few links with community groups	**Community Links**	Increase off-campus learning opportunities; Community participation policy; Community links database; Increase ventures with other community groups
Inconvenient times; No qualifications	**Resources for Learning**	Learning Centre open day and evening; Resource-based learning; Open college network credits; Unitised curriculum
Poor environment	**Environment for Learning**	Face-lift for reception areas; Refurbishment of classrooms and workshops; Learning Centres on main sites with access to IT
Irrelevant curriculum	**Design for learning**	More accredited courses at entry and level 1; Drop-in Learning Centres on both main sites; Flexible curriculum framework to give more choice; Helpful and supportive tutors
Perceived cost of courses; Negative local image; Unresponsive; Inappropriate marketing and publicity	**Information for Choice**	Publicise fee remission; Positive publicity in local media; Accessible information on flexible provision; Simple 'flyers' for targeted courses
More positive initial contacts; More personal contact; Guidance in early stages of enquiries	**Tutors for Personal Guidance**	Off campus drop-in centres for guidance with crèche; Learning bus offers guidance at regular venues; Friendly system for dealing with initial enquiries; Welcoming open reception areas

creating connections

Action

Three priorities for action were identified:

1. Gather information and build on college links with community groups

→ Community Links database developed

→ Community Participation Policy adopted following extensive and rigorous consultation

2. Increase opportunities for potential students to make friendly, supportive personal contacts with the College staff

→ active links with community groups to identify learning needs and requests

→ learning programmes and guidance set up in accessible local venues

3. Develop accessible information about the college to improve customer and staff familiarity with the college curriculum and progression routes

→ a 'credit framework' developed with a database of accredited units

→ a cross-college timetable devised to facilitate informed student choices

1. Gather information and build on college links with community groups

The College already had many links with the local community — particularly those forged through the Adult Foundation Studies

Division. The marketing team created a database of these and other links, to make information accessible for the promotion of new courses.

Considerable consultation informed the development of a 'community participation policy' for the college to ensure that this dimension was addressed in strategic planning. Several groups discussed the priorities and the principalship, heads of division, cross-college managers and the fellows produced a final draft which was endorsed by the College Governors in August 1996.

2. Increase opportunities for potential students to make friendly, supportive, personal contacts with College staff

Following the contacts established by the research, a number of community-inspired projects were established off campus. These included adult basic education with crèche facilities in a block of flats, a puppet theatre project with a group of Asian women, and photography and art workshops in association with a local housing project.

The 'Community Learning' Project

Linda is in her early 20s; married with three children, two at primary school and one aged three. Because there was a crèche, she was able to attend the 'Millmead Flats' project, run by a mature ex-student of South Bristol College. Linda left school at 16 with no qualifications. Her first connection with the college was the 'Family Learning' scheme, set up in April 1995 in partnership with community education and local primary schools. At Millmead she is helped with basic literacy, numeracy and using a computer, with the help and guidance of Kathy, an experienced tutor from the College. She plans to attend college for half a day each week to improve her basic skills work in preparation for an NVQ course in Child Care. She will need access to childcare facilities on the Hartcliffe site of the College to realise her hopes.

The college acquired and equipped a 'Learning Bus' with computers and information on learning opportunities and this is scheduled to provide regular guidance sessions in local venues. It has been successful in attracting local interest in education.

Through the work of the community-based projects, we could estimate that these initiatives have helped around 100 students to get back into study.

- The 'Fast Forward' programme which started in January 1996 enrolled 30 women

- the Millmead house project has enrolled between 20 and 30 people initially on to Adult Foundation Studies programmes and from September 1996 on to a variety of full-time college courses

- the Silai Textiles project enrolled eight and numbers are set to increase to 15 for the puppet-making work associated with this project

- the Inns Court Art project enrolled nine in March 1996 and in September 11 started a GCSE Art & Design combined with OCN level 1 & 2 credits

- a 'Parent Enterprise Training' course in Knowle Community Centre with 15 students

- the Learning Bus (funded jointly through South Bristol College and Bristol City Council) has also enrolled 20 people on to community learning groups

Each of these learning programmes has been requested and designed by local people in partnership with the college through the Fairbairn Fellowship and they are based in community venues.

To encourage participation the college has developed vocational/school link courses in partnership with 11-16 South Bristol Federation schools; the college is the natural progression route from them. Pupils are given a choice in years 10 and 11 to sample vocational areas such as construction, bricklaying, plumbing, painting and decorating, catering and motor mechanics, and develop skills which can be accredited. When they progress to college at 16 they will be able to use their earlier achievements towards gaining NVQ qualifications. This approach should encourage continued participation in learning.

Art and craft community-based learning project at Filwood, Bristol

3. Develop accessible information about the college to improve staff and customer familiarity with the college curriculum and progression routes offered

The credit framework

The focus of curriculum development was the implementation of the proposals in *A Framework for Credit (1995)* and the two FEDA sets of guidelines.

FEDA	NOCN	NVQ	GNVQ	GCE
Level 3	Level 3	NVQ 3	Advanced	A level
Level 2	Level 2	NVQ 2	Intermediate	GCSE A-C
Level 1	Level 1	NVQ 1	Foundation	GCSE D-G
Entry	Entry	LCCI		

The levels are cross-referenced to NVQs, GCSE and A levels. Level descriptors have been devised to distinguish between levels:

Entry level: allows considerable support from a tutor and records the learner's progress from their starting point

Level 1: allows some help and deals with simple, familiar situations

Level 2: requires the learner to be independent and deal with a range of familiar situations or concepts

Level 3: the learner is required to analyse a range of unfamiliar situations independently

These proposals require uniform description of the curriculum, breaking qualifications into units for the award of credit. Each unit has a level and requires 30 notional hours of study to achieve a credit in the currency of the system. Learning outcomes express the learning achieved, in terms of knowledge, understanding, skills, or attitudes. Assessment criteria are the quality statements used to assess the learning outcomes.

Implementation of a 'credit framework' to reduce barriers and to open up the curriculum has involved consultation and staff development. In 1994 a consultative programme brought together a wide range of staff with representatives from schools and community education to design a *Lecturer's Handbook for OCN Accreditation* and inform a *Monitoring Handbook*. This stimulated a demand for Open College Network (OCN) accreditation of courses. A management consultation exercise planned the strategy to embed the development of a credit framework in the planning cycle of the college.

A 'qualifications mapping' exercise plotted levels against FEFC curriculum areas to identify the gaps in provision at the College (see figure 8.2). This identified a need to establish a Level 2 and 3 framework for Access to HE courses some of which required revalidation. In 1995 an Access to HE programme with ten pathways was unitised and presented for OCN accreditation. In order to make all the units available for individual accreditation a **credit framework** programme was established, incorporating the Access to HE with 'unitised' A-level and GCSE subjects.

A major area for development was provision at entry and Level 1. The first courses were accredited in 1994: 'Work Options' at entry level for students with learning difficulties and 'Choices for Change' a return-to-learn course at levels 1 and 2 for learners with a wide range of abilities and aspirations.

In 1996 accreditation has centred on a 'Vocational Access' programme to promote participation and progression for school leavers with limited prior qualifications. This programme uses five strands of accreditation, showing how a credit framework can be used to draw qualifications together:

1 Further Education Award Scheme for Core Skills

2 London Chamber of Commerce & Industry, Entry Level NVQ in Vocational Areas

3 NVQ 1 Units

Figure 8.2: South Bristol College Qualifications and Credit Map 1994 - 96

FEFC Programme Area
None 0 ☐ Few <9 ▨ Many >10 ■

#	Programme Area	September 1994 Number of qualifications by FEFC Programme Area and Level				August 1996 OCN Credits by Programme Area and Level				September 1996 Number of qualifications by FEFC Programme Area and Level			
		E	1	2	3	E	1	2	3	E	1	2	3
1	Science, Maths & Computing	1	4	5	16		15	105	108	1	4	5	18
2	Agriculture									1	1		
3	Construction	4	3	2						5	3	2	
4	Engineering		2	10	8		2	8	8	1	3	11	9
5	Business Administration (inc IT)		10	22	19		2	26	27	2	12	24	20
6	Hotel & Catering (inc Leisure & Tourism)	2	3	3	1	8	8			4	3	3	1
7	Health & Community Care		1	8	5		1	41	48		3	8	7
8	Art & Design (inc Performing Acts)		1	4	8	56	59	68	24	1	2	7	10
9	Humanities (inc Education)		4	10	2	14	24	109	96	1	5	9	20
10	Basic Education (inc Return to Learn)	11	10	2	1	29	8	8	6	12	13	4	1

4   Open College Network accreditation for Art, Craft & Design
    Skills and Sport & Recreation

5   Foundation GNVQ in Business and Community Care

A wide range of programmes at all levels have gained OCN accreditation. Local interest in the award of credit has resulted in approaches from other providers to use submissions. In 1994 there were no learners gaining 'credits'; in 1995 154 learners achieved 'credits'; in 1996 there are over 500 learners registered for 'credit' award with 'Western Counties Access Partnership' (WCAP), our local OCN. While WCAP has given considerable support to the development of programmes, our participation has helped to develop a service responsive to the needs of learners.

The introduction of a credit framework in South Bristol has helped 676 students to gain OCN accreditation. This recognises achievements from a single credit for 30 hours of study on an introduction to information technology programme at entry level 1 or level 2, to the 25 credits at levels 2 and 3 achieved on a full access to higher education programme.

A 'unit database' is being developed on computer disk to make accredited college units available. The Welsh 'Credis' database is available on CD-ROM and the NCVQ database through the college computer network. The aspiration for students and staff to have access to a wide-ranging unitised curriculum for programme design is becoming a reality.

To improve the choices for students in designing their own learning experience a 'cross-college timetable framework' has been negotiated. This system aims to raise staff awareness of the opportunities to design individual learning programmes. The framework identifies a common pattern of 'time slots' and groups these in six 'blocks' during the week. There are three points in the year when new modules, or units start when students can join courses. This information is summarised on a few sheets of paper to enable staff to use the potential for creating individual learning programmes which combine more than one type of

c r e a t i n g   c o n n e c t i o n s

course. The sixth block is the 'F block' scheduled for all full-time students on a Wednesday afternoon to facilitate access to a wide range of learning opportunities across the curriculum.

The negotiations on cross-college timetabling mean that 800-plus students on full-time programmes can combine courses to have their own tailor-made programme. GNVQ Art & Design students can take A-level Photography, GNVQ Business Studies students can take AS level Law or Sociology. Wednesday afternoons have been made a time when all full-time students can choose from a variety of courses to enrich their studies. This choice includes retaking GCSE Maths in six months, pre-driver training, making jewellery, representing the college in sports teams, computer literacy, and drama workshops. These opportunities are open to all students whatever their age or the level of their studies.

Access to HE

Simon, a student in a wheelchair, enrolled on the general Access to HE course with the goal of studying Science, Society and the Media at the University of the West of England. The standard course includes core skills, psychology and sociology and was customised to include biology and Earth science. He has gained an Adult Learner's Award and a place at university.

A new college MIS student tracking system will be crucial in tracking achievement. This, and the structuring and coding of the curriculum will be central to facilitating a credit accumulation and transfer system. Accurate individual student records will help with rewarding all student achievement and attract funding for appropriate learning experiences.

Flexible delivery increasingly involves developing learning resources for accredited courses. Providing the writing, editing and publishing skills to produce quality resources is a challenge. A separate project is necessary to achieve this: four multimedia learning packages are being developed to support GNVQ Art and Design, Human Biology, a basic skills black history project and teacher training in teaching and learning styles. This work has benefited from connections with other Fairbairn Fellowships. For example, the Head of the Creative and Communication Arts was interested in producing a facility for producing in-house multimedia learning resources; discussions with Jette Burford at Halton College and Byron Lawson at Clarendon facilitated the development of a 'multimedia unit' at South Bristol College.

The Open Learning Centre provides access for the local community to develop IT skills or use computer aided learning

Evaluation and reflection

The current climate of external change has raised staff awareness of opportunities and threats and this can help with the introduction of local changes. In the last three years South Bristol College has experienced a microcosm of the general changes: redundancies, friction over new contracts, an unsuccessful bid for a single site in a converted building, the removal of the principal and, latterly, a merger to form City of Bristol College. Against this background colleagues have worked with the Fairbairn Fellows on the three main priorities to reduce the perceived institutional barriers to participation by:

- drafting a community involvement policy
- providing guidance and learning experiences off-campus
- developing a credit framework

Our experience demonstrates that enthusiastic commitment and effective management, including a detailed action plan, are needed to stimulate change in a college (see Figure 8.3 on page 98). The plan needs to include targets and performance indicators against which to measure achievement. We used the general theme of 'how will this improve learners' experiences?'. The objectives need to be broad to account for the varying success of different initiatives. The action plan, divided into eight areas, helped us to monitor and evaluate progress across this large and complex initiative. Setting priorities within the plan is essential for day-to-day decisions and ensures that key targets are wholly achieved, rather than a wider range partially achieved. The vital ingredient is to communicate enthusiasm for the project to colleagues.

The support of senior management has been an important element. The project was initiated by the vice-principal; a development budget allocated and the aims promoted.This helped to secure the commitment of many other staff. This has been an interesting job-share, bringing together a middle manager and a lecturer to initiate change: it has facilitated operating at a variety of levels across the organisation and contributed to our success in raising everyone's awareness of perceived barriers to participation. Both Fellows have achieved considerable personal development in their roles.

The advantage of a nationwide development project such as the Fairbairn is the range of friends, contacts and connections involved. They helped develop the multimedia project for learning resources in the college, the community policy and the off-campus guidance and

Figure 8.3: Overcoming the Barriers

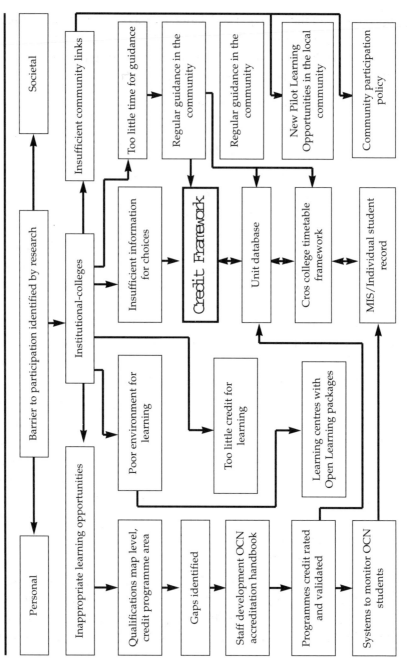

learning experiences. The contacts with other colleges working on the credit framework have helped increase our understanding of its implementation and application as a tool for curriculum design and quality assurance.

Within our area the major lesson has been that sharing and co-operation are more productive than competition in meeting the needs of learners. The Fellows have been networking across the college and the local community, raising awareness, internal marketing, acting as facilitators in developments, ensuring that ownership of curriculum and initiatives is with those who motivate learners. Everybody, including the participants, needs to own the changes so that everyone enjoys the fruits of learning and empowerment for progression. The considerable effort to gain new learners is essential and many will become lifelong learners.

Conclusion

Figure 8.3 (see page 100) illustrates how the project focused on the development of the credit framework. Barriers can be reduced by keeping the following priorities in mind when planning strategically to increase participation:

C	community links
R	resources for learning
E	environment for learning
D	design for learning
I	information for choice
T	tutors for guidance
F R A M E W O R K !	

Trisha Jordan is the Credit Framework Manager and Alison Shipton a Lecturer in Art and Design at South Bristol College, now City of Bristol College.

Bibliography

A Framework for Credit, FEU (1995), ISBN 1 85338 373 2

Framework Guidelines 1, FEU (1995), ISBN 1 85338 378 3

Framework Guidelines 2, FEU (1995), ISBN 1 85338 387 2

Chapter 9
Multi-tracking for resource and curriculum management

Richard Hopkins

South East Essex College

The concept of multi-tracking

Multi-tracking involves dividing the student population into a number of groups or 'tracks'. The academic year is modified in order to maintain the same number of days of student attendance at college as a traditional three-term academic year but attendance periods for each track are staggered so that at all times one group or track of students is having an 'off-track' session. Patterns of 'on-track' and 'off-track' sessions are arranged to suit the needs of the curriculum, with patterns such as two weeks of attendance, followed by one week of 'off-track' time. This allows for a significant increase in student numbers without similar additions to the resource base of the college.

For example, three tracks, with only two attending at any given time, gives a 50% increase in student numbers using the same teaching/ learning spaces and fixed resources.

The context of the multi-tracking project

In 1993 South East Essex College decided to apply for funding from the Esmée Fairbairn Charitable Trust to support a full investigation of multi-tracking and its application to FE. Senior managers at South East Essex College believed that great efficiency gains could be made through dividing the academic year into non-traditional patterns. The college was experiencing a rapid growth in student numbers, which was placing severe pressure on physical resources, especially accommodation. There was no immediate prospect of major new buildings.

Other innovatory developments were under way including a series of large open-plan learning centres but the idea of using multi-tracking to allow for continued growth in student numbers in existing accommodation, deserved a feasibility study, backed with a pilot scheme. (For information about accommodation developments at the college, see: *Altered Images: transforming college estates for a learning revolution* '— Innovations in FE 2, FEDA Spring 1995)

Open plan learning centre at South East Essex College

Developing a multi-tracking model for British FE

The project was conducted in two distinct phases. The first consisted of research into multi-tracking, leading to a report on its feasibility in further education. Feasibility having been established, the second phase of the project was authorised, a pilot stage to test the effectiveness of multi-tracking.

Over the three years of the project there were inevitable changes in emphasis. These resulted from the dynamic interpretation of the college's strategic objectives and the research findings. Particularly important was the development of a 'course-by-course' model of multi-tracking (as opposed to a 'whole-organisation' model as practised in the United States) which could feasibly be operated in the FE context.

This involved building 'tracks' from groups of students on the same course. It was then possible to plan in a very flexible manner, applying the concept to the most crowded curriculum areas. The two courses identified as potential pilots were a full-time course for adults called **IT for Work** which required extra IT workstations in order to accommodate extra students and a **BTEC National Diploma in Graphic Design**, a course mainly for 16-19 year-old full-time students which required extra printing and Apple Macintosh workstations. The course-by-course approach can be extended to as many or as few curriculum areas as suit a college's needs at any time. Figure 9.1 (see page 105) illustrates the three-track model applied at South East Essex College.

This flexibility was important to South East Essex College for two main reasons. In 1994 the college acquired a third major building, immediately reducing pressure on learning spaces. Far more significantly, it was developing new approaches to the management of learning; moving learning groups away from classrooms into open-plan general and specialist learning centres, where lecturers and support staff could operate in a facilitative rather than didactic mode. In these learning centres a very high level of information, communication and other technology is provided. Nevertheless, at times, demand outstrips supply and multi-tracking is an option available to managers. This flexible approach is consistent with college strategic objectives; multi-tracking as a management 'tool' to be used only when appropriate. The project moved the concept from the American school-based model concerned with classrooms, to an FE model concerned with greater efficiency in the use of expensive equipment. It was also important that, having established a contract of employment which allows for flexible deployment of staff, no new inflexibility should be introduced into the college environment.

Figure 9.1: Three - Track Model

■ Students On-Track   ■ College Closed   ▢ Staff Conference   ■ Students Off-Track

Week Beginning	Week Number	Track One					Track Two					Track Three				
		M	T	W	Th	F	M	T	W	Th	F	M	T	W	Th	F
4.9.95	1															
11.9.95	2															
18.9.95	3															
25.9.95	4															
2.10.95	5															
9.10.95	6															
16.10.95	7															
23.10.95	8															
30.10.95	9															
6.11.95	10															
13.11.95	11															
20.11.95	12															
27.11.95	13															
4.12.95	14															
11.12.95	15															
18.12.95	16															
25.12.95	17															
1.1.96	18															
8.1.96	19															
15.1.96	20															
22.1.96	21															
29.1.96	22															
5.2.96	23															
12.296	24															
19.2.96	25															
26.2.96	26															
4.3.96	27															
11.3.96	28															
18.3.96	29															
25.3.96	30															
1.4.96	31															
8.4.96	32															
15.4.96	33															
22.4.96	34															
29.4.96	35															
6.5.96	36															
13.6.96	37															
20.5.96	38															
27.5.96	39															
3.6.96	40															
10.6.96	41															
17.6.96	42															
24.6.96	43															
1.7.96	44															
8.7.96	45															
15.7.96	46															

The research phase

During 1994-5 research into multi-tracking investigated the 15 systems in use in the United States in 1993-4 and the 'extended academic years' and 'fourth-term' pattern proposed or operating in Britain, the United States and Australia. Field research was conducted in schools operating multi-tracking in California, and with representatives of the US National Association for Year-Round Education (which promotes multi-tracking) and the Los Angeles and San Diego County Offices of Education which are major operators of multi-tracking. Detailed discussions were also held at South East Essex College where 45 managers considered the effects multi-tracking would have on their management tasks. Research was also conducted with groups of applicants for courses at the college to establish their likely reactions.

It soon became clear that the American 'whole-organisation' model was inconsistent with the complex curriculum of smaller FE colleges so four variants of the 'course-by-course' model were demonstrated in detail, with two, three, four and five tracks, for courses of two to five groups. These accommodate and/or resource, respectively, between 20% and 50% more students. This can be seen in the chart indicating a simplified version of a three-track system. The resource efficiency is achieved through one group or track, at any given time, being 'off-track'. This is compensated for through a slight extension to the academic year, and, according to the type of course, the use of certain 'off-track' weeks for work set but not requiring full attendance at college.

The use of multi-tracking gave course managers new possibilities for curriculum enhancement. Art and Design staff devised 'Visual Research Projects' for students during 'off-track' weeks, using facilities in the wider environment rather than the college buildings. Staff delivering the **IT for Work** course assisted students to 'track-hop' by joining another track during some 'off-track' weeks, allowing adult students to arrange attendances taking account of responsibility for school-age children.

The pilot phase

The two pilot schemes operated in the academic year 1995-6. The first course was the full-time **IT for Work** course aimed at adults. Most students joining this course were unemployed and seeking to retrain. Three tracks were created, using two sets of IT workstations in a large open-plan IT learning centre which was used by these and several other groups of full-time and part-time students. Two case studies illustrate some typical student experiences.

Case study

Pam, aged 50, joined the third track, which started last. The 'delayed' start of the track particularly attracted Pam as a 'late' applicant who had half expected to be told the courses had all started and she could not join. She found the availability of 'track-hopping' attractive and took some time off to suit her childcare arrangements for her ten-year-old daughter, making up for this by joining another track on two occasions when she would have had 'off-track' time. She used other 'off-track' times to keep up to date and get ahead with her work by studying at home or by making use of drop-in facilities. Pam had no difficulties during the weeks on other tracks. This was because she found it easy to make new friends. This was less difficult than it might have been as the course was based in a learning centre and many of the faces were familiar already. She found the tutors very friendly and helpful and would recommend any course on a multi-track basis because of the flexibility. She concluded that 'the advantages outweigh the disadvantages'.

Case study

William, aged 21, was on the same track as Pam. Without any family commitments, he found the flexibility of multi-tracking unnecessary and did not 'track-hop'. The pattern of two weeks 'on-track' followed by one week 'off-track' time gave him unnecessary breaks. He would have preferred longer 'on-track' periods, possibly even four 'terms' punctuated with only short holidays. He did not consider 'track-hopping' to allow himself to 'fast-track' and worried that this would have involved him in too much administration. He did not fall behind with his work at any point so had no need to use 'track-hopping' to catch up or repeat. William could not say whether he would choose a multi-track course again but thought he would be more likely to if the 'on-track' periods were longer.

The **BTEC National Diploma in Graphic Desig**n course started operating on a multi-track basis in the second term, after a 'common first term' during which all Art & Design first-year students had 'taster' sessions. There were three groups of graphic design students, using enough specialist printing and Apple Macintosh equipment for two groups. A version of triple-tracking allowed for this resource efficiency. The experiences of two students illustrate some key issues.

Case study

Clare, aged 18, was on the first track. She had completed GNVQ Intermediate in Art & Design the previous year. Most of her friends were at college; very few were still at school. Her GNVQ course had been in its first year of operation and when she heard that her BTEC course was to be used as a pilot study her reaction had been 'guinea pigs again'. Her initial negative responses changed after the first Visual Research Project during an 'off-track' week. She enjoyed working this way because it gave her more personal control over planning and time-management aspects of her work. She found it hard to remember which 'off-track' weeks had been designated for Visual Research and which for vacation because she tended to do some work in her vacation weeks anyway, and found the Visual Research weeks pleasurable. Clare enjoyed multi-tracking overall, finding the non-traditional pattern a 'good simulation of being at work'. Her only problem was attending college 'on-track' sessions at Easter because the County Council would not pay her travel pass outside term time. The college assisted her with a payment in advance to cover her travel costs.

Case study

Jonathan, aged 16, on the second of three tracks, unlike Clare, did not enjoy multi-tracking. As a new student in the college , he missed not having the same holiday as his friends, most of whom were still at school. He did not mind the Visual Research Projects and was aware that although he had been encouraged to come into the college to see his personal tutor at least once for his progress to be monitored he had not done so. A plan to use 'track-hopping' was cancelled when his family's plans for a holiday fell through.

Conclusions

Multi-tracking proved to be an extremely flexible tool for managers who developed new approaches to the deployment of resources, both physical and human. It was most efficient when dealing with expensive, scarce equipment rather than (increasingly obsolete) classrooms. Its use during the pilot allowed 57 rather than 36 students to be accommodated on **IT for Work** and 62 rather than two groups of twenty on **BTEC National Diploma Graphic Design**.

Year	Course	Enrolments	Completions		Progression and Success Rates *
1994-5	BND GD 1	74	61	82%	97%
1995-6	BND GD 1	62	57	92%	100%
1994-5	IT for Work	23	19	83%	82%
1995-6	IT for Work	57	48	84%	77%

* Projections at 26th June, 1996.

As shown above, the pilot courses had no detrimental effects on retention because staff developed new ways of meeting students' needs. The staggered start dates also allowed managers to cope effectively with creating new groups when recruitment would normally have ceased. Multi-tracking is least popular with students who have had the most recent contact with school, but most students quickly adapt and a significant proportion find the challenges and flexibility beneficial. Managers at South East Essex College will continue to use multi-tracking on a selective basis as a proven additional method for resource and curriculum management.

Richard Hopkins is the Associate Director for Curriculum at South East Essex College.

Chapter 10
The Fellowship has made a difference...

increasing participation to meet community needs

Caroline Miller and Sarah Rennie

Northumberland College

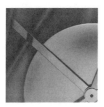

On the right, going north, just before Scotland

Most people only know vaguely where Northumberland is. Even to Northumbrians our College was simply known as 'Ashington Tech' even after incorporation three years ago. The main College campus is in Ashington, an old mining town in the south-east corner of the vast county of Northumberland. Inland from Ashington lies a huge area of beautiful but sparsely populated hills with some of the most spectacular scenery and history in Britain. The less happy side of Ashington is its present level of unemployment: 12% with pockets of up to 30% in the area around Ashington. Few major employers are found outside the south-east corner. What work there is focuses on small or medium-sized firms. Transport is expensive and communities away from the coast and the main A1 road to Scotland are poorly served by a rural bus service.

...and beyond

Although our College no longer offered Mining Studies, very little had changed in 1993. We still expected most of our students to make the long journey to Ashington to join taught classes or particular courses. True, there was a small annexe at Berwick-upon-Tweed, nearly 60 miles away on the Scottish border, where a few office skills courses took place and we were slowly learning about marketing courses to businesses, but 'going to College' still meant travelling to the monolithic building in Ashington.

The new College mission statement began to change that perspective:

> To provide education, training and services of quality to the region's community, its business and beyond.

Added to this, our first strategic plan provided a new sense of direction, a direction which included the bid for a Fairbairn Fellowship. We decided to share the Fellowship between two members of staff, one with a background in information technology, the other from adult education. From the start, this imaginative approach has been reflected in the way

creating connections

the College has used the Fellowship to make sense of the mission statement, particularly that enigmatic phrase 'and beyond'.

What can we do?

From the outset people have been at the heart of the Northumberland College Fellowship. We have involved staff and students across the whole College and from a wide variety of backgrounds and communities. In educational terms our aims were ambitious:

- to enhance the learning experience of part-time students
- to increase the participation of students throughout the county in learning programmes
- to promote the flexibility of learning programmes

In real terms, these aims were translated into action by choosing people rather than systems as our focus. The systems were there only to enhance the experience of the people. We included ourselves as part of the system and chose to allocate a relatively small part of the Fellowship funding to the equivalent of a half-time post between us. Most of the money has been spent providing other people with time to develop ideas for learning resources for students.

If only we had time...

The three years of Fairbairn Funding allowed us to:

- fund staff to write learning materials
- send people to staff development events aimed at flexibility through the use of technology
- support the first tentative steps in delivering courses at outreach centres such as Amble, a small fishing and industrial town on the coast 12 miles north of the main College

- fund support staff in a training programme which led to 13 staff gaining NVQ level 3 in Customer Care

In all, over 60 staff and more than 200 students have been directly or indirectly involved in the Fairbairn Fellowship-related activities. It is through this wide involvement that the Fellowship has made its impact on the College.

I didn't realise curriculum development could be so creative...

Five Fairbairn mini-projects, each with its own project manager, were established in four of the College's programme areas, including Health and Social Care, Information Technology and Science.

The projects shared a high level of commitment to the Fairbairn themes of access, participation, flexibility and technology. We were constantly surprised by what could be achieved by the right person, with the right ideas and the right support. By the end over 30 workbooks, support materials and study packs had been produced and have been used already by more than 150 students in college, at home, in the new centres and at work. Many more will use them next year.

It is a happy atmosphere... I enjoy it

One of most exciting aspects of being a Fairbairn Fellow has been watching the centre at Amble grow up like the ugly duckling. What began as a small project sponsored by the TEC and the local high school, with only minimal College involvement, has become a thriving local centre for the College with a wide range of courses already on offer and more to come next year. There are approximately 220 students enrolled at Amble and related smaller centres.

Early on in the Fellowship students and staff at Amble asked for beginners' IT. The constraints on numbers, space and computers meant that a traditional class would not be viable so the College's open

Students enrolled for beginners' IT

learning model was used instead. This gave each student 15 minutes of contact time per week; the time was pooled to provide tutorials at different times in different weeks to try to meet the needs of all the students.

The students used the materials developed on the project and very quickly the numbers grew as word went around. It is very striking that in the right environment, adult students with no recent experience of learning can use IT to give them the start they need.

'...I was pleasantly surprised how the course is run, in that each student has a set of objectives and can work as fast or as slow as s/he feels fit.'

'An attractive feature is undoubtedly its flexibility. I am in full-time employment and would have missed quite a few sessions under the old system, but now I can attend when possible and stay for the whole day, if I so wish.'

Medical practice receptionists were also having difficulty arranging to have sufficient time released from work to attend the Association of Medical Secretaries and Practice Administrators and Receptionists (AMSPAR) course. Thus, another of our mini-projects was born and up-to-date flexible workbooks were developed for this group of students. According to the programme area leader, as well as allowing this group to successfully complete their programme, the materials developed have been invaluable on a number of other courses and have allowed her to rationalise timetabling and realise efficiency gains that were never envisaged at the start of the project.

Who or what made the projects work?

The projects fostered the development of teams of different kinds; in Science the subject specialists began to work as a whole team reviewing much of their approach to the delivery of the curriculum in response to

Teamworking

the common issues of low recruitment and the ensuing non-viable class sizes, while the languages project brought the staff involved into much closer contact with learning resource centre staff and core (key) skills specialists.

But time is of the essence...

We have learnt how important the overt support of the line manager is in any project of this nature. For instance, the Science project was not only ongoing throughout the last year, but it was also always included as an agenda item for team meetings and the line manager always pushed the team to ensure that they never let it move down their list of priorities.

Our own support has also proved to be important in the success of projects, both on a one-to-one basis and at the joint meetings which lasted way beyond their scheduled length because everyone wanted to talk about what they were doing. The opportunity to share this sense of excitement with colleagues from different curriculum areas was valued by everyone.

However, the real key to success is to give staff time and overt recognition for the innovative work that they are doing. None of our project managers was given anything like as much as they gave in return.

I need to be able to work at home

At the main site we had identified a need for a laptop computer hire scheme aimed not at the IT student but at those who wanted to type up assignments, for personal use or just to feel more comfortable with using a computer. With some trepidation we purchased six laptop computers and software, set up a hire agreement, worked out a hiring system via the Learning Resource Centre and then advertised the service. Nothing happened! Was the £25 deposit putting people off? Was the weekly

creating connections

charge too high? Was our research wrong? The scheme was intended to be self-financing over two years — was this unrealistic? Just as we were about to reduce the price the scheme took off and never looked back. We've had our problems — viruses, people changing the software and so on. These are now resolved and there is almost always a waiting list and a cry of 'When will you be getting more?' Now that we know it works there will be more both in the College and at the outreach centres.

Case study

Two years ago we considered the plight of Joan, a mature student from Berwick. For all of her programme bar one day of keyboarding skills she had to travel to the main site. Joan had two options for this — either the College bus or to use her own car. Travelling by the College bus meant leaving home at 6.45 a.m. and not arriving back home until 6.35 p.m., but it was free. If she used her car then the length of her day was reduced to just 8.5 hours, but it cost her £10 per week.

Initially Joan did not think that she would stick the course, but her determination saw her through. What of the student without her resources or with a young family? If Joan came to the College now she could study much of her programme at Berwick using up-to-date facilities and IT equipment. For the parts of her programme not delivered there face to face she could use videoconferencing to communicate with her tutors and peers.

The most liberating aspect of the Fairbairn Fellowship was that we were given the freedom to develop the project as we felt was most appropriate within the framework of the original proposal. This has allowed us to take on board the changes and developments which have occurred within FE and the College itself over the last three years. The project has been so closely linked to the College's strategic plan that often it has been difficult to clearly distinguish the Fellowship activities from other College initiatives and this has also ensured support from our senior management. These are the factors which have been the most important key to success.

What next?

Early on in the Fellowship we had a vision of truly taking the College to the community, and how better to do it than to take a classroom on wheels to the remote towns and villages of the county. A bid was prepared and in the last three months the funding has become available and planning for our travelling classroom has moved from the 'grand idea' to a rather daunting reality. Plans are being discussed, quotes sought and strategies decided upon.

Another strategy for taking the College into the community is to establish videoconferencing in three outreach centres and, via the travelling classroom, into village halls using money from the successful competitiveness fund bid. We believe that this will allow students from all over the county to gain real face-to-face contact with other students and/or their tutor without having to travel long distances to the main site. As our Director of Curriculum stated, 'Videoconferencing was made for Northumberland.'

One of the three outreach centres

We have taken every opportunity to benefit from the Fairbairn Fellows network with visits to other colleges and in particular, gaining a head start when introducing programmes using videoconferencing with some excellent staff development from Halton College in the effective use of the virtual classroom.

As for the Fellows

The three years of the project have flown by with alarming speed, but we have made lasting friendships with other Fairbairn Fellows, we have learnt an enormous amount and have had tremendous fun along the way. We will both feel a deep sense of satisfaction if we can believe that we have helped to make a real difference to the communities of Northumberland. That can only really be judged by our peers and by those who are served by Northumberland College.

Caroline Miller is the Curriculum Co-ordinator and Sarah Rennie, the Learning Resource Centre Manager at Northumberland College.

Chapter 11
Increasing access and participation

Ruth Ardron

Wakefield College

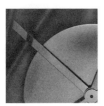

Introduction

The Wakefield College Fairbairn Fellowship Project aims included increasing access and participation for the long-term unemployed in an area suffering high unemployment due to the decline of the mining industry. They also incorporated staff development, curriculum development and community development.

'Go out and multiply the student enrolments,' said the Finance Director to the Fairbairn Fellow at the start of the Project in 1994. Despite having previously enjoyed a variety of challenging roles within the college including establishing courses for the unemployed, and co-ordinating open learning, the task in hand seemed daunting in the climate prevailing in 1994.

'Panic, panic!' screamed the Fairbairn Fellow.

'Where will those additional "bodies" be found?'

'How will that increased access and participation be achieved?'

The Fairbairn Fellow's nightmares gradually reduced as the project outcomes were achieved and the evidence produced indicated not only increased participation involving 719 adult students, but many more community, college and international networks and developments. Upon reflection, the Fairbairn Fellowship project work became more and more hectic, but also exciting and fulfilling. The developments initiated will be embedded in the college structure as a reminder to the staff and students of the additional training facilities and venues in the Wakefield District which may be attributed to the Fairbairn Fellowship project.

Developments initiated and delivered since the start of the project in January 1994 include:

i) Training provision at community venues:

- Featherstone
- Upton
- South Kirkby

ii) Open learning provision for the unemployed

- materials development for use in community venues
- intensive keyboarding skills (Word)
- word processing (Word 6)
- Excel for Windows
- Access Database
- Powerpoint

Open for Learning project established in community venues

- Featherstone Library
- Knottingley Library
- Five Towns Resource and Technology Centre

iii) International links

- flexible learning training programmes delivered for teachers and managers from The Netherlands
- ERGO 2 (Minergon Project) — a comparative study of training for the unemployed in the former East Germany and Italy

Marketing and publicity

At the outset, a Wakefield College Fairbairn Fellowship Monitoring Group, chaired by the Principal, John Muskett, was established.

Members of the Monitoring Group also included:

- Faculty Director: Continuing Education, Communications and Languages
- Assistant Directors: Adult Education, Access, Library and Learning Resources, Enrolments, Student Progress
- Staff Development Officer
- International Manager
- Marketing and Publicity Manager
- FEU (now FEDA) Regional Development Officer
- Fairbairn Fellow

The Fairbairn Fellowship Monitoring Group has met at least once a term throughout the project and has proved an essential management framework for the staff, allowing their expertise to be fully used.

During the first few months a marketing and publicity plan was devised and implemented to publicise the college's success in achieving a Fairbairn Fellowship award and to raise Fairbairn awareness. The publicity materials included Fairbairn Fellowship leaflets and display boards. There were press releases in the local newspapers and the college newsletter. Publicity venues for the display boards included the three college centres, local libraries, Jobcentres and the Wakefield Metropolitan District Council Centres for the Unemployed.

Publicity materials were also distributed to local, national and international contacts. Marketing and publicity has been a continuing feature of the Fairbairn Fellowship, both within the college (faculty meetings and staff development sessions) and at external events.

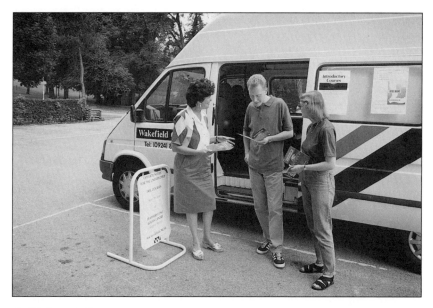

Publicity minibus

After the initial plan was implemented a more specific marketing strategy was devised to target the unemployed adults in the community. This coincided with promoting four-week introductory courses at a Featherstone community venue in June 1994. At this stage the Fairbairn Fellow took to the road and used a college minibus as a publicity tool at various community locations in Featherstone including the market, library and the adult education centre. Leaflets and posters were delivered personally to Jobcentres, shops, rugby clubs, doctors' surgeries, housing offices, schools and community centres — wherever potential recruits might be targeted face to face. The results of this intensive marketing were 75 student enrolments and a near smile from the Finance Director!

Following the success of the Featherstone introductory courses, similar provision was planned during December 1994 for Upton, a village 12 miles from Wakefield with high unemployment caused by the decline of the mining industry. Open Days were held at the Upton Village Hall and college staff promoted the training provision and crèche facilities at Upton during the New Year.

To coincide with the pre-Christmas festivities, additional activities were arranged at open days held in the Upton Village Hall, including:

- crèche facilities for the children
- Father Christmas/gifts for the children
- College jazz band performance
- refreshments (for all visitors)

Additional funding had been obtained from the Training and Enterprise Council (TEC).

Networking

Networking has been another crucial element of the Fairbairn Fellowship both within our own organisation and outside it. It has been encouraged by the Fairbairn Fellowship Steering Group and group meetings arranged with the Fairbairn Fellows.

Agencies

Additional funding has been essential from the beginning and has contributed to successful initiatives, which might not otherwise have been possible. The Coalfield Project Officer of Wakefield TEC was invited to visit the Featherstone introductory courses. This led to a request to establish similar training and crèche provision in the Upton community with funding from the Coalfield project.

Networking with other organisations has also proved to be an important complementary feature of the Fairbairn Fellowship. Networking with Wakefield Metropolitan District Council, Upton and North Elmsall Parish Council and Wakefield Libraries have all contributed to the successful implementation of the community provision.

Achievements

Following the introduction of the Upton Village Hall New Skills Programme and the students' demand for additional courses, it was soon realised that the funding allocation would not meet the local demands. Networking arrangements with the local agencies resulted in a successful Single Regeneration Budget bid for skills training in Upton and South Kirkby, which will provide funding for the Upton/South Kirkby project until March 1997.

Wakefield College is committed to responding flexibly to the educational and training needs of the community by maximising opportunities for achievement and success. This commitment has been endorsed by the recent conference at the college for agencies and individuals working to promote the development of the Wakefield area and its people.

Working with colleagues from Wakefield library, the district council and Wakefield TEC, the college now provides an open learning consultancy service in preparation for the launch of the Open for Learning provision in Featherstone and Knottingley libraries. College lecturers provide tutor support in the community to unemployed adults who use the open learning materials to achieve qualifications.

Fifty-five unemployed adults are now studying a range of subjects including GCSE English, A-level English, GCSE Mathematics and Supervisory Skills (Introductory Award/Certificate) through open learning.

Successful networking with the Manager of the Five Towns Resource and Technology Centre in Castleford has also resulted in some students taking advantage of the Open for Learning project. The students receive tutor support from college lecturers in the Five Towns Centre for the NEBSM Supervisory Skills, a subject not offered to the adult unemployed under the course provision of the centre. Networking with the staff and students has also provided the Fairbairn Fellow with an opportunity to discuss college provision for adults and to increase awareness of opportunities by organising group visits to the college centres.

International developments

Further networking has resulted in the delivery of four flexible learning programmes for lecturers and managers from The Netherlands. The Fairbairn Fellow has provided an opportunity in the programmes for the visitors to witness the flexible provision and learning methods offered in the Fairbairn Fellowship project. During a reciprocal visit to The Netherlands it was very satisfying to see the implementation of flexible learning language training for the adult unemployed and other similar developments taking place.

A successful bid to the European Commission for an Ergo 2 (Minergon Project) has provided further opportunities for networking with international partners in Italy and the former East Germany. An application for the Ergo 2 (Minergon Project) was made to the European Commission shortly after the award of the Fairbairn Fellowship but not granted until July 1995. During the last few months a comparative study of the training programmes for the unemployed at Upton, Cottbus, Germany and in Ancona, Italy has been carried out. The locations were selected in view of their similarity to the Wakefield area in relation to high unemployment caused by the decline of industry. The results of the Ergo 2 are currently being disseminated and, it is hoped, will help local, national and international organisations in future programmes.

Project outcomes

The Wakefield College Fairbairn Fellowship Project aimed to increase participation from the long-term unemployed through community development, curriculum development and staff development.

Community development

The Fairbairn Fellow has actively worked with organisations in Wakefield, including the TEC, Economic Development Department of the Council, Wakefield libraries, and Upton and North Elmsall Parish Council to ensure community developments were made in accordance with local needs.

Factors considered included the unemployment trends within the Wakefield District and the relevant training needs as identified in a report on the South Elmsall, South Kirkby and Upton local needs audit by the Policy Research Unit at Leeds Metropolitan University. This report identified that:

- 53% of the population, aged 16 or over, had no qualifications
- one per cent of the population possessed a degree
- 32.1% of the residents were interested in undertaking training and education

Marketing has been a key feature of the community development and has involved liaison with the College Marketing and Publicity Manager in devising plans and materials for the promotion and dissemination of the Fairbairn Fellowship locally, nationally and internationally. Promotional events in the community have included open days, a film premiere promoting the Upton video *Meeting the Needs of the Unemployed*, a certificate presentation, an Open for Learning Exhibition and community network meetings.

Many of these events relate to the developments which have taken place at the Village Hall in Upton, where training/education was non-existent and a high rate of unemployment prevailed.

The community development work has been disseminated to a wider audience at conferences: **Meeting the Needs of the Unemployed; Working with the Community** held in Wakefield.

Further dissemination will take place with national and international agencies using the video and a checklist circulated for completion. The

creating connections

checklist includes topics relating to establishing training provision including:

- networking with other organisations
- accommodation for programme delivery
- marketing/publicity/recruitment
- funding for course delivery
- training payment to students
- qualifications offered
- progression routes

An analysis of the findings will be circulated to the organisations involved in providing training provision for the unemployed.

ii) Curriculum development

Prior to the promotion of training for the unemployed in the local community venues (Featherstone and Upton) consideration was given to the Local Needs Report in relation to the retraining needs of the unemployed. The introductory programmes offered included: Exploring English, Exploring Numeracy, First Aid, Information Technology (Featherstone) and the Introductory Certificate in Supervisory Skills.

The essential feature of training provision at this initial stage was to remove the barriers to returning to a learning environment. Short introductory courses were timetabled within school hours (9.15a.m. — 3.00p.m.).

Most of the students enrolled had no previous qualifications and lacked confidence. It was essential to provide a student-centred approach where adults could study at their own pace in a user-friendly, non-threatening, accessible environment and enrol throughout the year. This was done in most subject areas by the use of flexible learning materials.

First Aid students in action at Featherstone

Following the success of the introductory courses at Featherstone the adults were integrated into the existing adult education provision already available at the centre.

The success of the introductory courses at Upton led to greater student demand, and the need for more resources. Hence the need to secure additional funding by means of a Single Regeneration Bid to acquire more accommodation and equipment within the village hall, and funds for extra courses, as well as the supporting créche facilities.

At the outset of the programme, the village hall was used as a classroom and the council chamber as a créche. To increase the accommodation two storerooms were converted into one computer classroom and a Portakabin from the college was built on to the Village Hall and equipped as a purpose-built créche. This freed the council chamber for use as a classroom.

Students using the adapted computer room at Upton Village Hall

Since September 1995 the range of subjects offered has included:

- Beauty Therapy
- Business Administration
- Childcare
- Confidence Building
- Counselling Skills
- English (basic and GCSE)
- Information Technology
- Mathematics (basic and GCSE)
- Law
- First Aid
- German
- Health and Hygiene
- Supervisory Skills

A qualification is offered in all subjects and students may enrol on a weekly basis. Workshop provision in some subjects (English, Mathematics and Information Technology) and the use of resource-based learning materials, increase flexibility. Other subjects are offered on a modular basis, where students may enrol at the start of a module. For example, Childcare modules require attendance for two hours for six weeks.

Advice and guidance are provided throughout the year and Careers Guidance sessions are also provided at the Village Hall. Progression is encouraged and organised group visits are made to the college centres.

For those unemployed adults who prefer to study by the open learning method, facilities are now provided at two community libraries and at the Five Towns Resource and Technology Centre. The Open for Learning provision at the libraries includes a display of open learning packages and the use of equipment (computers, video and tape recorder). College lecturers provide the tutor support to the students in the local venues.

Not only have the students in the Wakefield community gained from the flexibility provided, but our partners in The Netherlands and other countries are interested to learn about our provision.

Staff development

An extensive programme of staff development sessions is offered to college staff throughout the year. This includes subject-specific topics, technology, curriculum development methods and personal development. Staff development sessions have been provided by the Fairbairn Fellow on **Working with the Unemployed**. Staff are also updated on the Fairbairn Fellowship developments at the faculty meetings attended by all staff. College newsletters are circulated to all staff and include Fairbairn Fellowship updates.

A Continuing Education Faculty Community Network group has also been initiated which brings together the community development in the Wakefield area.

Increased participation and achievement

Since the start of the Fairbairn Fellowship specific course codes have been devised which identify students enrolled as a result of a Fairbairn Fellowship initiative. A total of 719 student enrolments have been recorded to date. This figure includes those students enrolled at community venues, e.g. Upton and also those students who have progressed and enrolled at the College.

The qualifications gained by those students to date include 235 certificates with an additional 58 examination results currently awaited.

Not only has the Fairbairn Fellowship project provided an opportunity for community development, curriculum development, staff development and the associated quantifiable increased student participation and achievement, but the qualitative outcomes have been recorded through interviews with the students at Upton Village Hall and the video *Meeting the Needs of the Unemployed*.

At the outset the Fairbairn project entitled *Increasing Access and Participation* seemed a daunting challenge, but it has proved to be most exciting and rewarding for all those involved, even the Finance Director.

Ruth Ardron is the Community Initiatives Manager at Wakefield College.

Chapter 12
Access to open learning for deafblind adults

Lynda Sharp

The City Lit Centre for Deaf People

1. Existing provision at the City Lit Centre and its association with the voluntary sector

In 1994 the Fairbairn Fellowship offered us the chance to develop a more co-ordinated system of support for deaf students with additional visual impairment. Formerly there had been occasional association between educational bodies and voluntary organisations for deafblind issues. There are few deafblind people in the country but even so the term covers a range of conditions including hard of hearing with partial sight; and partially deaf with partial sight; profoundly deaf with partial sight; partially hearing with severe vision loss. At the City Lit Centre we encourage students to consider how they should describe their sensory loss to others outside the Centre.

We were able to tackle four key areas: resources, teaching methods, equipment and IT, which staff had repeatedly highlighted through assessment, review and curriculum evaluation.

The three major organisations in the voluntary charitable sector with whom the City Lit Centre works most closely are:

- Royal National Institute for the Blind (RNIB)
  RNIB services maintain registers which include deaf clients. People who lose their sight in early life develop functional skills which can disappear again if their hearing is affected in later life.
- National Deaf Blind League (NDBL)
- National Deafblind and Rubella Association (Sense)

These links mostly take the form of exchange of information and advice involving staff from the respective organisations.

Apart from local social services, the Centre's teaching staff and the deafblind students' families have been the key links for communication and in relaying information. Beyond the Centre and the three organisations, sensory functions tend to be taken for granted — easy communication and observation are not generally considered until some tribulation occurs. A sudden illness, irreversible injury or unrecognised progressive impairment in the prime of a 'normal' life interrupts the spontaneous course of study or vocational training.

2. Communication skills at the City Lit Centre for deaf people

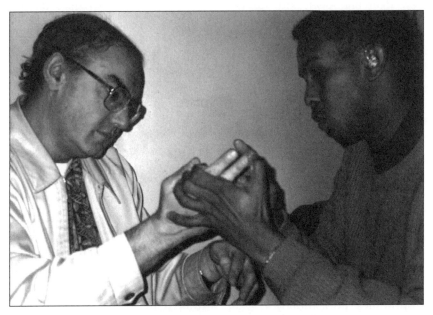

Hands on British Sign Language/Signs Supporting English

Deaf and Deafblind adults use widely different types of communication including:

- lipreading, speech and amplified hearing
- lipreading and Signs Supporting English (SSE)
- lipreading and British Sign Language (BSL)
- lipreading and Hands-on BSL/SSE

- BSL as first language (exposed to BSL in early childhood/prelingual)
- BSL as second language (either after established oral English or other home languages)
- speech and BSL/SSE

Few deaf and deafblind adults are completely alike in their use of communication methods.

Speech or sign language?

The Centre staff are skilled at meeting a student's preference for communication in British Sign Language (BSL) or Signs Supporting English (SSE) or spoken English. Many students are keen to enrol for Speech Therapy knowing that with their limited or intelligible speech, they may or may not have potential for improvement. However, if the students are able to express themselves more effectively in BSL or SSE the staff proceed accordingly.

Each student wishing to enrol in the Deafblind Workshop is first assessed on their ability to study independently. Social skills and personal maturity are observed during personal interview and conversation with staff and other students. All enrolled students in the Continuing Education for Deaf Adults (CEDA) programmes are, however, encouraged to participate in groupwork. Deafblind students, because of the nature of their disabilities do not take part in groupwork without the assistance of a communicator.

Where a student wants a tutor for one-to-one work, staff reduce the dependency by using tactics such as pair work and brainstorming exercises with groups or the whole class. On average, five students attend the weekly workshop in the Computer Centre where there are eight PCs available for up to five hours each Friday. Isolation in hostels or families through lack of communication skills is minimised when the student builds confidence through new relationships at the Centre.

Many students are eager to converse with others outside the classroom but some, during breaks, retire into their own world, munching on their sandwiches, content to sit alone in the crowded canteen knowing that soon they would be communicating with ease back in the classroom. Staff encouraged these students to get more acquainted with other students in the workshop. Fostering the desired contact was a slow process but some progress became apparent after several weeks.

Two of the students took at least a term to feel confident about approaching another student on their own. They both use speech and lipreading to communicate in the hearing world. Encountering deaf people using sign language was a new experience for them and use of tactile communication came as a surprise. Several weeks went by before they became accustomed to the use of Hands-on SSE.

Fingerspelling and deafblind manual alphabet

It is not easy to describe in written language how and what fingerspelling is and why it is used frequently in communication among deaf/deafblind people and between deaf/deafblind and hearing people. Visual demonstration with videotapes and software disks are needed to introduce definitions and description. Attempts to demonstrate how a living, moving language works, using fingerspelling, manual and non-manual features in the printed form will certainly bemuse the reader.

Anyone unfamiliar with these techniques should adopt a new perspective when observing two people communicating at ease together. One or both of the people may be deafblind. Deaf and hearing people develop skills to communicate with deafblind people. These involve tactile use of hands and arms which we refer to as Hands-on Sign Language. Fingerspelling is the action of spelling out words, letter by letter, in rhythmical styles which represent intonation much as the voice does.

The continuum of communication modes used by hearing people in the business world include: television presentation, radio, public speaking, interviewing, interrogating, lecturing, instructing and so on. Style, vocal intonation and expression change according to situation, ranking and protocol. Sign Language operates in equivalent but different ways — it is not merely a means of survival with only basic vocabulary and aimless gestures. The art of conversation flourishes in sign language as well as in spoken language around the world. BSL is a systematic, rule-governed language with its own grammar and lexis. This applies to sign languages in other countries such as American Sign Language (ASL) and French Sign Language (FSL).

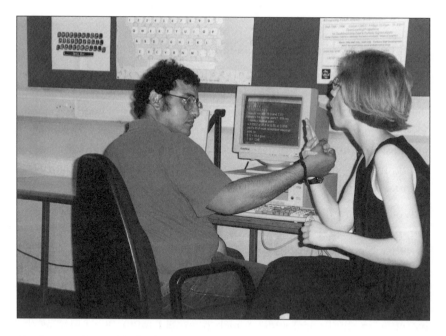

Teacher working with deaf student

3. Embedded courses at the City Lit Centre

Based around the needs of deafblind learners and the range of skills on offer at the Centre, the Fairbairn Fellowship development project delivered three courses, targeting three different groups of people.

a) Access to open learning workshop for deafblind adults

The pilot workshop for deafblind adults took place in June 1995 and led to the formation of a weekly workshop programme in September 1995. Research and survey assignments were carried out over eight months, concentrating on one geographical area, due to transport difficulties across local authority boundaries. Transport is a crucial factor as mobility allowances and councils' disabilities transport policies are all local. Although publicity was restricted to target areas, information reached other regions.

Six students enrolled on the pilot course which extended over four consecutive Fridays and lasted for 20 hours in total.

Students in the target group have:

- partial-to-severe vision loss. Any useful sight depends on the environment and the tutor's use of accessible resources
- partial, severe or profound hearing loss
- had normal vision during childhood and have established some visual perception which has been maintained after sight decline

Most of the students have Usher's Syndrome. The National Deafblind and Rubella Association (Sense) defines Usher's Syndrome as 'a genetic condition which causes deafness from birth and sight loss over a number of years. This sight loss often begins in late childhood and is caused by an eye condition known as Retinitis Pigmentosa (RP). RP is a major cause of severe visual impairment in people under 40. Its early symptoms include difficulty seeing in the dark and in different lighting

Figure 12.1: Overview — The City Lit Fairbairn Fellowship Project:

What are the teaching objectives in the Deafblind Workshop?

Information Technology:
Perform key commands, work with computer jargon, set up page layouts, experiment with colour and text points, transfer data between disk and drive, build up competence with touchtyping, evaluate accessibility and usefulness of software, evaluate hardware for improvement in future development.

Communication Skills:
Take initiatives by approaching staff and other students for help; explore achievable approaches by using different communication methods with staff and other students; state preference in use of equipment and resources; access relevant information, verbally or written, set by staff or by teaching resources.

What were the available resources?
Staff - full-time academic, part-time hours, training budgets, specialist skills: project manager, project development coordinator, subject lecturers, assistant IT tutors, administrative assistant.

Technology
Had to work within given constraints of The City Lit CEDA provision and external consultation.

How do we ensure project is integrated to bigger picture?
• Linked Keeley House Centre to the City Lit main IT base network
• Embedded the Fairbairn Deafblind Workshop into the Centre's programme and prospectus

Linked to other CEDA programmes:
• Adult Basic Education
• RSA English/Maths
• City & Guilds GCSE/NVQ
• National Skills Profile
• CACDP

Ways forward for improved access and teaching approaches
• Fairbairn Network with FE, HE, AE and Art Tech colleges in UK
• Assess and evaluate the video resources
• Marketing to exceed special educational needs field.

• Use Deafblind programme in CEDA curriculum as springboard assessment and workshop option
• Partial sighted students in mainstream City Lit/external programmes receive additional one to one tuition
• Obtain appropriate equipment for use in all learning environments, i.e. magnification software
• Person hours for adapting worksheets and storing on disks

c r e a t i n g   c o n n e c t i o n s

Maths:
Specific learning goals to be negotiated with individual students according to ability, need and interest. Examples from the first year of workshop include ability to convert between metric and imperial units; ability to convert between currencies (given conversion rate); ability to simplify algebraic expressions
Aims: To maintain existing skills and knowledge and increase them so as to function more efficiently in areas of daily life where numbers are important. To explore areas of subject at appropriate level. To attain next level, by examination or assessment, of their chosen career or personal academic path.

English:
Specific learning goals to be negotiated iwth individual students according to ability, need and interest.
Aims: To enable each student to build on existing language skills within the constraints of their disabilities. To explore ways of developng language skills using any media helpful for the students, using new media and technology where appropriate.

Financial
- Project Manager: CEDA Head of Unit oversees running cots of project development, teaching hours and timetable schedules
- Co-ordinator: ensures development tasks are achievable within budget constraints

Materials
Existing lanaguage resources' bank versus those needed (adapted, enlarged, updated)

Ongoing links with external agencies:
- CACDP Touch 'n' Go Project
- RNIB Education & Information
- SENSE Usher Project
- PATHFINDERS Mental Health
- Liaise with Social Services in Greater London Boroughs
- Liaise with employers for day-release enrolment

Ongoing links with external programmes
- NVQ Business Administration Level 2
- Higher Education degrees
- Commercial IT

Set clear performance standards and SMART objectives with goals
- SPECIFIC
- MEASURABLE
- ACHIEVABLE
- REALISTIC
- TIMELY

- Recording work on disks and project formats
- Printed materials used in all courses to be put onto disks and a clear contents index to be maintained (for easy adaption)
- Equipment resourses which can be used for all sites/rooms: CCTV, computers, Braille equipment/software, magnification software

conditions. Over time, vision gradually deteriorates until tunnel vision develops'.

Some students use British Sign Language or a spoken language, other than English, as their first language. Some students have retained speech even with declining hearing, a common feature of deafness; partially deaf children lose further hearing in adulthood, with or without their knowledge.

The workshop was devised as a discrete springboard for open and flexible learning approaches. Some students are now enrolled on both discrete and integrated courses. There will always be students who can only enrol on discrete courses where there is a low staff-student ratio.

The weekly timetables for deafblind students in the Access to Open Learning Workshop were devised to accommodate four subjects: English, maths, keyboarding and communication skills. These were the four subjects requested in the 1994 survey of social services and voluntary sector organisations with deafblind clients. All the returned questionnaires described communication skills as essential/crucial to improved contact with families, friends and local services.

Figure 12.1 provides a summary of the key features of the open learning workshop for deafblind students.

b) Staff Development — CACDP Touch 'n' Go Deafblind Communication & Guiding Skills Level 1

The Council for the Advancement in Communication with Deaf People (CACDP) was formed in 1981 to enable professional workers to gain qualifications in communication and interpreting skills. A CACDP vocational programme was initiated at the Centre in the same year. The development of these staff development courses and the open enrolment programme described in 3c were a natural addition to the Centre's portfolio.

The City Lit Institute and the Centre for Deaf People, including the Continuing Education for Deaf Adults Unit (CEDA), have an established ethos of staff development within which staff training is a priority. Academic, clerical and caretaking staff were offered Council for the Advancement in Communication with Deaf People (CACDP) accredited training with priority given to the staff members having immediate contact with deafblind people. The training involved raising awareness about issues and causes of deafblindness, the importance of communication, different methods of tactile communication and guiding skills, use of simulation and role-play. Subsequently, all teaching and front-line reception staff became qualified deafblind communicator guides.

c) Open Enrolment — CACDP Touch 'n' Go Deafblind Communication & Guiding Skills Level 1

The CACDP 'Touch 'n' Go' project developed curriculum and guidelines to enable professional fieldworkers to work efficiently with deafblind clients. Greater awareness of safety, for example, is expected for those who work as guides, social workers, care workers, volunteers and befrienders. Families and relatives enter the Touch 'n' Go courses to enable them to care for their deafblind member with greater understanding. Ideally, health-service workers and doctors would benefit from this understanding. The Open Enrolment programme supported by the Fairbairn project includes the following CACDP Courses in the Sign Language Training Unit Programme:

- CACDP BSL Stage I — Beginners level
- CACDP BSL Stage II — Intermediate level
- CACDP BSL Stage III — Advanced level
- CACDP/NVQ Level 5 in Interpreting British Sign Language (*from 1997*)
- CACDP Deaf Awareness

- CACDP Touch 'n' Go Deafblind Communication & Guiding Skills Level I

4. In the classroom with resources and technology

In conjunction with the weekly workshop, attention was turned to the development of resources. There is an existing language resource bank at the Centre which is constantly revised and restocked. All worksheets needed to be enlarged and their layouts adjusted. The CEDA team, full- and part-time, are skilled in creating worksheets on a daily basis due to the paucity of suitable education materials for adults with poor language acquisition.

We improved the resources and developed the curriculum week by week. Layout of worksheets and enlargement of text had to be devised before any actual teaching and learning took place. Tutors in CEDA work out the accessible format of materials for deaf students with additional impaired vision in all curriculum areas.

Within the deafblind workshop, the existing available Windows WRITE programme formed the base of all keyboarding worksheets. Students saved all their work on their own floppy disks.

Shortcut command keys were taught rather than use of the mouse which proved impractical without a magnified insertion cursor.

The magnification software found most accessible was:

- Dolphin-Lunar and Zoomtext for IBM compatibles
- InLarge for Apple Macintosh

To date, there is shareware software available for an enlarged mouse pointer but not the insertion cursor.

Students are encouraged to experiment with colour schemes and size of print. They all discovered that reading print on paper differed from reading on screen. Visual impairment prevents easy reading on the default white screen so we used a selection of colours, texts and frames to accommodate all needs.

Students need training to use the closed circuit TV (CCTV) effectively with their study and coursework. In-built powerful magnified lenses with monitors enable people who are able to read enlarged print to use a personal computer and other network systems. A basic worksheet gives a student with limited field of vision maximum access to further study and enables independent judgement of their own progress.

The weekly timetable is divided into four one-hour sessions, covering English, maths, computer and communication skills. Students are first interviewed and assessed on their preference of subjects.

The workshop operates on the basis of one-to-one tuition. Some students enrol for all the subjects and others pursue only the minimum of two subjects, generally computer and communication skills. Groupwork is possible only when each participating student has an individual communicator.

Computer and Communication skills include work-related coursework. Standard instructions on applications for work-processing, database and spreadsheets are adapted with vocabulary building exercises, business English and social/office skills.

Materials used in the workshop include exercises on technical terms, jargon and working relationships in business and training programmes. Computer manuals are not available in large print so staff transfer data to worksheets with enlarged print and diagrams.

5. What difference has Fairbairn made at the City Lit?

Since the beginning of the Fairbairn Fellowship, extensive professional training brought about significant awareness raising about the needs of deafblind people in colleges. I made some innovative inroads with other departments at the City Lit Institute which brought about renewed confidence between myself, the deafblind students and other staff. Other colleges made contact with the City Lit to explore further funding to enable access for deafblind adults in their regions. Deafblind adults in various regions also responded enthusiastically to my questionnaires often adding comments appreciative of the fact that finally recognition of their needs is being taken up.

Work with deafblind people necessitates, in most instances, a high staff/student ratio. This has obvious budget implications and the use of trained volunteers will lower costs in the longer term. Modifications to the building, in terms of decoration were identified, e.g. staircase threads/risers painted white, wall/door/doorframes painted in light/dark tones. Some of these have been addressed, but more still needs to be done.

In hindsight, more emphasis should have been placed on the informal partnerships developed during the Fellowship - especially that which involved us with the CACDP 'Touch 'n' Go' Project. Established links between CACDP and the Sign Language Training Unit could have been usefully extended to the Fairbairn project. The competitive ethos which seems to prevail between organisations, charitable or otherwise, did not help the notion of partnerships. Because of an apparent lack of clear guidelines, the concept of matched funding appears to be only loosely applied.

6. The future — post-project

a) Outcomes

The Deafblind Open Learning Workshop is in full operation at the City Lit Centre for Deaf People and Speech Therapy.

The City Lit learning resources manual *Working with Deafblind adults in Further and Adult Education* (working title) will be published in late 1997. Contents will include: guidelines, practical teaching approaches, techniques and use of learning resources.

Access with the Network: CEDA is included in the City Literary Institute Network system along with enrolment, library resources and mainstream computer studies. Access to Internet and e-mail for further and adult education studies would not have been achieved without Fairbairn's role in breaking down barriers for marginalised adults.

b) Recommendations for future research and development

Technology costs should not deter development of continued access for students with visual impairment. Commercial technology investors are recommended to make use of AE community centres in rural and urban regions to run trials and quality testing.

Learning provision for deaf and visually impaired people can be substantially enhanced by:

- provision of standardised magnification features for CD-ROM, multimedia and the Internet
- sponsoring projects (curriculum, technology, resources and management) for local AE community centres in all regions

7. The Fairbairn Fellowship

Originally, there were two co-Fellows nominated for the City Lit Fairbairn Fellowship: one specialising in technology development and the other Fellow, being profoundly deaf, with links to the 'grassroots' deaf community. Six months into the Fellowship, staff changes at the City Lit led to the appointment of just one full-time Fairbairn Fellow. British Sign Language communication skills proved to be advantageous within the Fairbairn Fellowship. This was perhaps the first time that all the Fairbairn Fellows had a professional relationship with a profoundly deaf person.

Lynda Sharp, the Fairbairn Fellow involved, is a lecturer in deaf studies and communications skills at the City Lit Institute.

Chapter 13
Integrating multimedia flexible and open learning into the curriculum

Bill Lockitt

Coleg Llandrillo
Llandrillo College

Introduction

In October 1993 Llandrillo College put forward a bid for one of the Esmée Fairbairn Fellowships. At that time, it was a case of looking three years into the future and trying to anticipate the types of learning environments, systems and needs of a modern learning society. Today, the fruits of this work are integrated into many of the college systems and delivery methodologies.

A great deal of interest has been stimulated by the results of the Welsh Fellowship and its effects have not been restricted to the local community. In 1996 we take for granted many of the things we could only dream about in 1993. Which came first, the chicken or the egg? Has the vision formed reality, or has reality caught up with the vision?

The experience of managing the Fellowship at Llandrillo College has highlighted the importance of identifying clear aims and objectives from the start of a project and modelling the desired outcomes. The model may, and probably will, alter as advances are made but it provides a benchmark for evaluation and modification. It is also clear that providing time to develop these learning models, and investing even small amounts of funding, can make a discernible difference to existing practice, both locally and nationally.

The rapid expansion of further/adult education and training, coupled with new and exciting methods of delivery and assessment methodologies, will require the same level of innovation, planning, managing and modelling as the Welsh Esmée Fairbairn Fellowship.

In 1970 Toffler attempted to put the speed of change into perspective and produced the following paradigm:

> '...if the last 50,000 years of man's existence were divided into
> lifetimes of approximately 62 years each, there have been about 800
> such lifetimes. Of these 800, fully 650 were spent in caves. Only
> during the last 70 lifetimes has it been possible to communicate
> effectively from one lifetime to another — as writing made it possible

creating connections

to do. Only during the last six lifetimes did masses of men ever see the printed word. Only during the last four has it been possible to measure time with any precision. Only in the last two has anyone anywhere used an electric motor. And the overwhelming majority of all the material goods we use in daily life today have been developed within the present, 800th, lifetime.'

Toffler, A. (1970)

The changes taking place today are far more rapid and complex than those of the 1960-70s and are affecting all areas of society. The development of FE/AE/HE within a modern learning environment will require a new breed of management. They should not be afraid to challenge, change and develop existing educational systems and develop a curriculum framework that is relevant to the needs of a global society.

The Llandrillo College Fellowship

Although a number of projects were undertaken during the Fairbairn Fellowship four main projects brought together all the aims and objectives of the original bid.

'To develop multimedia, flexible and open learning to attract those who would not normally use Further or Adult Education'

- the development of a comprehensive cross-college CD-ROM, Computer-Based Training (CBT), Computer-Assisted Learning (CAL), including Internet and e-mail access

- Internet and e-mail network

- the introduction of flexible learning centres and learning bases

- Open Learning support via Info-Net and Prospects 2000 partnerships

- the use of new technology to support open and distance learners

After the initial identification of needs and several months of discussion, two developmental models emerged, one for learning bases and learning centres (see model 1), the other for open learning (see model 2).

Learning centres and learning bases/college-wide learning network

Using the concepts of learning centres (cross-curricular) and learning bases (curriculum-specific) the college has developed a network of flexible environments. Students can drop in informally and access

Learning Bases and Learning Centres: Model 1

Student tracking and quality control systems — Area staffing

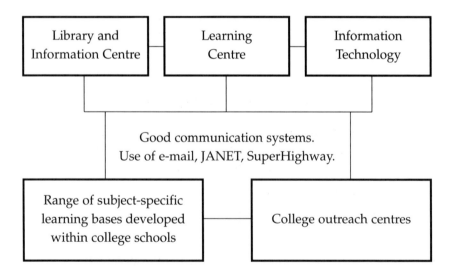

Multimedia Flexible and Open Learning Materials

Open Learning Model used at the College: Model 2

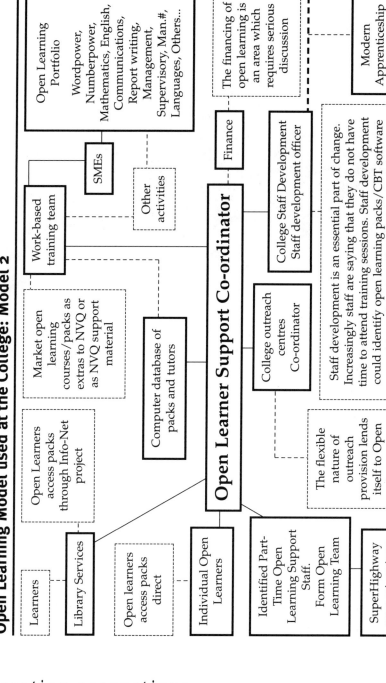

Open Learning Portfolio

Wordpower, Numberpower, Mathematics, English, Communications, Report writing, Management, Supervisory, Man.#, Languages, Others...

The financing of open learning is an area which requires serious discussion

Modern Apprenticeship core skills

SMEs

Work-based training team

Finance

College Staff Development
Staff development officer

Other activities

Staff development is an essential part of change. Increasingly staff are saying that they do not have time to attend training sessions. Staff development could identify open learning packs/CBT software and issue this to staff with identified needs

Market open learning courses/packs as extras to NVQ or as NVQ support material

Open Learner Support Co-ordinator

College outreach centres Co-ordinator

Open Learners access packs through Info-Net project

Computer database of packs and tutors

The flexible nature of outreach provision lends itself to Open Learning

Learners

Library Services

Open learners access packs direct

Individual Open Learners

Identified Part-Time Open Learning Support Staff.
Form Open Learning Team

SuperHighway support systems

Llandrillo library and information resource centre

learning materials, resources and assistance. The facilities are also duplicated in a range of outreach centres dedicated to offering support within the community.

Three learning centres have been developed within the college:

- **the learning centre:** Mathematics, English, Communications, Basic Skills and GNVQ key skills

- **the library and information resource centre:** a cross-college resource dealing with teacher training, staff development, open learning and library/information services

- **information technology:** a drop-in centre integrated into all curriculum areas

New staffing methodologies have been used in the learning centres and the opening hours have been extended by using a combination of learning facilitators and timetabled lecturers.

CD-ROM, CAL, CBT and Internet access are provided via the college network and are some of the supportive features of the learning centres.

A student survey in June 1996 highlighted the following comments about the learning centre:

- 97% thought the environment satisfactory to excellent
- 93% thought the paper-based material satisfactory to excellent
- 98% thought the computer-based learning material satisfactory to excellent
- 97% thought the support in particular curriculum areas satisfactory to excellent
- 98% thought support on computers satisfactory to excellent
- 98% thought that the support offered met their individual learning needs
- 97% thought that access to learning materials was satisfactory to excellent

The questionnaire also asked students to make comments on what they enjoyed about the centre:

- helpful staff/help on demand
- good working environment
- good resources
- space
- CD-ROM access
- 'drop-in' resources
- excellent support

There were, of course, areas in which the learners wished to see improvements but these concentrated around systems and technology rather than delivery. Some of the areas are in the table on page 162:

Learners' needs	College responses
More access to the Internet	*FE-Net Wales project will provide full access to the Internet in September 1996. All students using the net will be provided with recognised qualification via NWAC validated units.*
More books and other learning material	*New £2.5 million library to open in September 1996 with access to local and wide area networks. Full networked CD-ROM / CAL / CBT software.*
Better communications systems	*All learners to be provided with e-mail addresses as of September 1996. Will also have five Mb set aside for individual information and work. Communications learner to learner, learner to tutor and tutor to learner.*

Both students and staff have welcomed the introduction of learning centres and learning bases.

Open learning and the introduction of new delivery methodologies

The needs analysis undertaken during the first two months of the Fellowship highlighted the need for open/distance learning support. It was clear that if the students were to benefit from open learning, any scheme could not be confined to Llandrillo College. And so the concept of a 'North Wales' partnership arrangement emerged.

After discussion with senior librarians and college principals, a comprehensive partnership 'Info-Net' was formed in 1994. A network of five colleges, county libraries (now all new authorities), the local TEC (TARGED) and Marcher Sound radio was created.

This partnership is committed to open learning support. As well as developing cross-county support for open learners using material via the libraries, all colleges have, or are about to launch, individual open learning schemes that will be integrated into the college curriculum delivery. Since its launch in February 1996, the Llandrillo College open learning support scheme has attracted 250 new learners to the college.

The quality and comprehensive nature of the open learning support offered in North Wales was recognised in May when the scheme won the 1996 National Open Learning Award (NIACE/NEC).

The model used to develop open learning is shown in Model 2. Learners can enter the model via their local libraries or directly via college admissions. A comprehensive open learning database has been developed and this identifies relevant open learning materials, qualifications available via the Welsh Fforwm database of Open College Credits (OCC) and if tutor support is available. Only when a learning package, accredited learning outcome and a tutor have been identified will the support system become operational.

The database also allows the college to identify gaps in learning provision and log all student enquiries. This information is used to purchase materials or identify areas that need qualification aims.

Open learning information is also given to the college commercial and work-based training section. It is also playing an increasing role in staff development, particularly in the area of new technology.

People helped by the Fairbairn Fellowship

The local area network

The Llandrillo College CD-ROM network was one of the first Fairbairn projects and the initial pilot of ten multimedia computers in the College library set the foundations for future developments. Today there is a sophisticated Wide Area Network (WAN) with over 300 multimedia computers connected, not only on the main site, but also to three of the outreach centres. The WAN is used by all the students (10,500-4000 FTE) on a regular basis and greatly assists in the learning process. The college have also been able to maximise the potential of the Welsh FE-NET project and now have full e-mail and Internet access for all staff (350) and students (10,500 full-time and part-time).

The open learning support project

The Info-Net project brought together five colleges, five of the new authorities and the local TEC (TARGED). It has helped hundreds of learners to access education and training via the library services. It has also helped to form closer partnerships with local colleges.

The PROSPECTS 2000 open learning support project (based at Llandrillo) has helped several hundred learners since its launch in February 1996 and won a national NIACE/NEC 1996 award.

A new open learning unit within the library is opening this autumn to service the needs of business, industry, SMEs and individuals through North Wales, with plans to extend this service to learners outside the UK.

Staff development

At least 60 college staff have attended staff development events focused on integration of new technology into curriculum support. On a personal note, I have been asked to speak at over 20 conferences and represented Wales at a four-day open learning conference in Tampere, Finland in October 1995. The theoretical basis of this work has been provided by my part-time Ph.D. on 'individual learning styles and the design of intelligent learning systems'. This research is attracting interest from both educational establishments and industry.

Students using open learning facilities

Conclusion

As stated in the introduction, by injecting a small amount of funding the Esmée Fairbairn Fellowship has freed up time to address needs affecting not only Llandrillo College but also open learning and networking of CD-ROM/CAL/CBT in Wales and nationally.

A few of the measurable identified outcomes of the Fellowship are:

	1994	1996
Open learners at Llandrillo	0	230
Networked CD-ROMS (new network July 1996 capacity 150 to 200)	0	100
Networked multimedia machines	0	300
Open Learning partnerships	0	12
Multimedia college prospectus	0	1
Identified Open Learning material (college-based)	0	130
Identified Open Learning material (county-based)	0	1300
Open Learning database matching credits/materials/tutor	0	1
Open Learning support tutors (part time)	0	199
Open Learning courses offered by the college	0	40
Networked CBT/CAL packages	0	20

The development of learning centres and learning bases has also been undertaken as part of the Fellowship and is now continuing within the college. The Welsh FE-Net project will also assist in phase three of the open learning project by helping new technology to support business, industry and small and medium-sized enterprises (SMEs) via the Info-Net partnership.

Educationalists currently have the opportunity to develop a radical new model of education which will take society confidently into the year 2000 and beyond. In order to achieve this transformation, some reverse engineering is required. The type of future we want for our new 'global village' must be identified, the key skills and knowledge requirements highlighted and the systems put in place which will deliver the required outcome.

Technology is only part of the answer. The ancient Greeks achieved outstanding results with very few mechanical aids; they thought that 'the mind was a splendid tool, one of the most delicate, and potentially one of the most precise instruments that one could imagine' (Downey, 1964). This is still the case today. All we need to do is use it.

Bill Lockitt is the Flexible and Open Learning Manager at Llandrillo College.

Bibliography

Elliott, K./Lockitt, W.G. (1994) **Credit based developments and flexible technical workshops at Llandrillo** Staffordshire Open Learning Unit

Kolb, D.A. (1984) **Experiential learning** Prentice-Hall I, ISBN 0-13-295261-0

Lockitt, W.G. (1994) **The implications of multimedia flexible and open learning for the management of modern learning environments** QTP Ltd

Lockitt W.G. (1996) **Developing open learning at Llandrillo College** Llandrillo College

Logan, R.K. (1995) **The fifth language — learning a living in the computer age** Stoddard

National Institute for Adult Continuing Education **Life-Long Learning in Wales — A programme for prosperity** NIACE

Toffler, A. (1973)   **Future Shock** Pan Books ISBN 0-330-026818

White Paper on Education **Teaching and Learning - Towards the Learning Society** HMSO, 9-28275698

Wales Regional Technology Plan **An Innovation and Technology Strategy for Wale**s Welsh Development Agency, Cardiff

Chapter 14
The key messages of the Fairbairn
Fellowships

Ursula Howard

FEDA

Our travelling classroom has moved from the 'grand idea' to a rather daunting reality... Videoconferencing was made for Northumberland'

Northumberland College

Structured research applied to practical models in a real community provided us with unique results

Halton College

'Creating connections' was the phrase which seemed to the editors of this book most neatly to encapsulate the work of the Fairbairn Fellowships from 1993-6. Many other key concepts and practices have flowed into this distillation. Ruth Gee has provided a full account of the origins, the vision and the management of the Fairbairn Fellowships from beginning to end. This chapter will seek to pull together from the range of individual projects, some of the essential ideas, characteristics and outcomes of this major initiative and point the way towards further work.

In 1955, the Principal of Royal Salford Technical College wrote that a 'danger exists in that ... we may entirely neglect research into our own work'. (Venables, 1955). It was also noted that 'research and investigation in its own fields of study' was 'another service to the community which the technical college should fulfil'. The calls in the 1950s were for research into selection and placement of students, the problem of low standards in mathematics, educational and vocational advice and guidance, women's education and teaching in a skills-based sector. There was emphasis then, too, on the vital importance of further education for economic survival and the need to promote flexibility and quality for the 1,360,000 students in further education — 'Unexamined traditional methods.... will no longer suffice'. There was 'an ever-increasing need for change'. The book continues to elaborate an eerily prophetic theme in astonishingly familiar language. It is sobering to remember that FE will always face the need to respond to economic and social change. As the Llandrillo College Fellow noted, the pace of change

c r e a t i n g   c o n n e c t i o n s

this century has been discontinuous with the past. Since 1955, a nation still enjoying full employment, although 'on the threshold of the automatic factory in the atomic age' (ibid) has entered the post-industrial and post-atomic age. We already live in a society in which information and communications technologies are profoundly transforming the way we work, and live. Communication has become paramount. What is different now from 40 years ago is reflected in the title of this book and its central concerns.

The Fairbairn Fellowships Scheme is probably the first ever sustained and coherent effort at a national (UK-wide) level to promote research and development activity in FE. It is significant that the first qualitative requirement of the Esmée Fairbairn Charitable Trust in setting up the scheme was that proposals should be 'imaginative and original'. The primary focus of the fellowships was 'the development of the FE curriculum, utilising new ideas of flexible learning and modern learning technology in order to help achieve measurable increases in participation, attainment and learning productivity'. In the FE sector, where research is critically underdeveloped, the fellowships provided an opportunity to learn the skills of action research, to develop a new 'product' and to implement it. Each project tackled a nugget of work from broad themes on which colleges were crying out for a coherent set of messages at local, regional and national levels. The Fairbairn Fellowships have provided at least some answers to two key questions. First, what are the key factors for colleges in improving participation, attainment and more effective learning? Secondly, what role can flexible and open learning, using new technologies play in such improvements?

These were burning questions for colleges seeking growth in 1993. They are even more crucial in 1996. Colleges are urgently looking for the means of sustainable growth in a financial climate of more for even less. At the same time they are genuinely seeking to widen participation to groups of people such as those who have not achieved qualifications before, have not participated in post-school education, or who have learning difficulties or disabilities. A further group is identified by

Fairbairn - those in each of these groups who may be apprehensive about new technology or even technophobic. Achieving growth for these groups in these circumstances at the same time as investing in new technologies is not an easy task.

Fairbairn's lessons will be useful, although some of them may not be new or surprising. But they will be a helpful contribution to the development of FE because they are rooted in practice and describe in practical detail how the Fellows worked towards their aims. They have provided detailed accounts, relevant information and a formal record of the projects and their diverse contexts. As such they provide a rich resource for colleges wishing to embark on research projects. Some projects have resulted in high quality, innovative products. The Stevenson College resource pack is a case in point. The following paragraphs seek to draw out the key issues and messages which have emerged.

The first key message is the importance of co-operation. The Fellowships were set up and managed as a partnership, with continuous peer-group learning between Fellows built into the structure of the scheme. This was mirrored in the projects themselves. The importance of co-operation between projects and mainstream college activity and between colleges and other bodies is strongly emphasised. The examples of Clarendon, Halton and South Kent Colleges and the Northern Ireland projects demonstrate the tangible benefits of partnership and co-operation in reaching new learners and at the same time attracting new funding.

Secondly, the fellowships have shown how much can be achieved on relatively little. As the Llandrillo College Fellow wrote: 'providing time to develop these learning models and investing even small amounts of funding can make a discernible difference to existing practice, both locally and nationally'. In other words, there is a cumulative effect in harnessing local effort to a wider national project. This kind of coherence is often lacking in educational research at all levels. Funds for research in FE are essential, but with proper planning there can be economies of scale and benefits gained which are disproportionate to the funding of individual projects. The total value is greater than the sum of the parts.

Thirdly, there is a message about the capability of staff in colleges to ride the tidal wave of change which colleges have experienced since the publication of the White Paper on Education and Training in 1991 which led to incorporation. The 'product development' and action-based approach of the projects demonstrate the capability of many staff in FE to grasp opportunities and work to maximise small resources. The Fellowships have prefigured some of the work proposed by the FEFC's Committee on Learning and Technology (Higginson) (FEFC, 1996) , the Tomlinson Committee on SLDD (FEFC, 1996) and the Kennedy Committee on Widening Participation (continuing). They have caught the wave of the Competitiveness Funds as it broke. Wakefield College's project exemplifies how co-operation from an international level to the micro-community can attract significant extra funds and support. EU funding was achieved for partnerships with Italy and the former GDR. The local TEC's Coalfield project enabled créches and complementary training. Networking with the parish councils led to bids for Single Regeneration Budget funding.

Modern, technologically supported provision in village halls, council chambers and mobile units — linked to learners in other countries and (potentially) continents — also raises issues of time and space. Fourthly, then, there is a strong element of 'back to the future' in the lessons of Fairbairn. The effectiveness of the concepts and values of outreach and community development, meeting the needs of local people wherever they can learn, or feel comfortable learning have been clearly restated, even rediscovered by the Fellows. However, new technology has enabled models for a new kind of community education to develop. Old village halls hum with the 'white heat' of the newest technologies. And the most local provision can also be the most potentially universal. For example, people videoconferencing in their community centre in south Kent or Cheshire may gain more direct and authentic experience of French life and language than learners in college classrooms or language laboratories.

Old forms of learning in the community, which have strong roots in informal groups such as nineteenth century mutual improvement societies, find new life and meaning through open and flexible learning using telematics. Grassroots associations have always flourished best when they could provide what people wanted and needed to learn in their own chosen time and place. New technology and regular analysis of needs in the community make it easier for colleges (big institutions) to serve local needs flexibly as they arise and to respond when they change. Flexibility was a key focus of Fairbairn's research brief. It has proved possible to break up the rigidities of time and space which inevitably accompany provision in large buildings with set timetables.

If there is an irony in finding that the way to the future is through best practice in the past, there is also a welcome paradox in the point made by Jette Burford in the preliminary analysis of the Halton College project: the most disadvantaged, marginalised learners in terms of educational background, achievement and mobility positively enjoy learning at the cutting edge of technology. This is the fifth key message. As the City Lit's project for deafblind students noted, 'breaking down barriers for marginalised students' has led the way to Internet access and e-mail for all the unit's students. In some cases technology can provide quite simply the difference between access and exclusion. This is exemplified by this project's recommendation for standardised magnification features for CD-ROM, multimedia and Internet. Fairbairn has positive messages for approaches to 'inclusive learning', the key concept of the Tomlinson Committee.

There is some evidence that non-traditional learners are not more likely to drop out of courses using new technology in teaching and learning, for example videoconferencing. There is even evidence that these learners find community-based models using telematics less intimidating than classrooms. They offer more independence. A related point, from the Stevenson College study, is that the right blend of human contact, information and advice with access to technology, matters most in breaking down barriers and moving from 'technophobia' to 'guarded enthusiasm'. The Fellows are right to be cautious in generalising from the findings of one local project. However, their work reinforces the view that further research is needed into how people learn through technology and how it can motivate learners. We also need to know more about the possible links between different learning attainments, learning difficulty on the one hand and learners' attitudes to and success with flexible and open learning centred on new technology on the other.

The sixth key message of the Fairbairn research is the importance of a clear management framework in the college to support a research and development project in further education. Such a framework, where it is clearly present, enables the effective monitoring and evaluation of projects which is essential to their credibility. It brings benefits which come from a clear commitment to the project by the senior management team. Where the projects are effectively managed, the messages can clearly flow into the cycles of strategic and action planning. If research in FE is to flourish, or be taken seriously as a contribution to the development of education and training as a whole, it is essential that it is built into the framework of planning. An example of this from Fairbairn is the way in which the findings of research and development can focus staff development activity. The potential for boosting learners'achievement by developing staff competence and investing in staff time for innovation is clearly demonstrated by a number of Fairbairn projects.

Furthermore, FE colleges are well placed to ensure that research projects are focused and well managed. In FE, management culture is strong relative to other sectors. The growing culture of quality assessment, evaluation and team effort, are clearly focused on the strategic plan. There is a framework to ensure that research funds are well spent. There is a growing need for research into FE, which is becoming more widely recognised. There is an inadequate knowledge base from which to take key decisions. The stakes are high. The wrong strategic direction or tactical approach to the challenges a college faces can be costly. However with a small injection of research funds, the payback to the organisation and to the nation could be high in terms of increased participation, achievement and standards. The achievement of the National Targets for Education and Training lies substantially in the hands of FE. Explorations such as the Fairbairn Fellowships show how quickly new learners can be won to FE if the approach is systematic and timely. Another lesson of Fairbairn, then, is that it is worth investing in the FE sector: it is more than willing to work in partnership with higher education and other partners in a much needed strategically focused research effort.

A seventh message is that one small piece of informed innovation can inform the direction and scope of the wider curriculum. Declining subject areas may not be moribund. The example of Shrewsbury college demonstrates how science provision, which has suffered falling numbers, may be re-energised by identifying new approaches and techniques and targeting new groups of potential learners. Science in particular is a case where the long-term national interest may be in conflict with current consumer demand and funding pressures. Colleges may be caught between the two. The results of a research and development project such as the 'Science Centre' may enable colleges to take a decision which will serve both short-term and longer-term interests, at institutional and national levels.

The final key message I want to bring out is the importance of going back to fundamental questions about access, achievement and how people best learn. The South Bristol project, for example, began with the big question: 'Why did relatively few local people take up learning opportunities?' With this information they could then move on to the complex questions of how to improve access and experiment with innovative solutions. They chose the development of better co-operation in the community and the implementation of a credit system to help learners better understand the curriculum and progression routes. It is interesting to relate this approach with the multi-tracking system at SE Essex. Both aim for user friendliness, but adopt different approaches. Each has the dual purpose of efficiency and better access. This process of open-ended investigation, practical experimentation, development and evaluation is new for the FE sector. Clearly it has not been uniformly implemented nor uniformly successful. But where the story of a project is clearly told and well-supported by evidence, this book is rich in information, recommendations and results from which others can learn.

Each Fairbairn project will be evaluated. However, it will be important to evaluate the Fairbairn Fellowships as a whole. Innovation takes time to take root and grow. It takes time, as individual researchers noted, for a centre equipped with the latest technology to be set up and launched. The real difference which Fairbairn has made will therefore take time to establish conclusively. But the value of such a model has been proven: adequate and positive answers have been provided to the two key questions posed above. The model will hopefully be extended and honed to provide a solid basis for research in FE. The sector needs continuing innovation and new information to prepare for the 21st century. The Esmée Fairbairn Charitable Trust has sown seeds which have flowered. If the FE sector can provide a climate in which such work can grow, institutions and learners would reap the benefits.

Ursula Howard is the Director of Research and Information at the Further Education Development Agency (FEDA).

References:

1 Venables, P.F.R. Technical Education: its Aims, Organisation and Future Development, London 1955

2 Higginson, Gordon (1996), The Report of the Learning and Technology Committee, FEFC, 1996

3 Tomlinson, Prof. John (1996), Inclusive Learning — the Report of the FEFC's Learning Difficulties and/or Disabilities Committee, HMSO 0113613415

4 Education and Training for the 21st Century, HMSO, 1991

Cmnd 1536 — vol. 1, 0101153627

Cmnd 1536 — vol. 2, 0101153627